SYNTACTIC STRUCTURES REVISITED

SYNTACTIC STRUCTURES REVISITED

CONTEMPORARY LECTURES ON CLASSIC
TRANSFORMATIONAL THEORY

Howard Lasnik with Marcela Depiante and Arthur Stepanov

The MIT Press
Cambridge, Massachusetts
London, England

This book was set in Times New Roman by Asco Typesetters, Hong Kong and was printed and bound in the United States of America.

Library of Congress Cataloging-in-Publication Data

Lasnik, Howard.
  Syntactic structures revisited : contemporary lectures on classic transformational theory / Howard Lasnik with Marcela Depiante and Arthur Stepanov.
      p.   cm. — (Current studies in linguistics ; 33)
  Based on tape recordings made in the fall of 1995 of a portion of a syntax course taught by Howard Lasnik at the University of Connecticut.
  Includes bibliographical references and index.
  ISBN 0-262-12222-7 (hc : alk. paper). — ISBN 0-262-62133-9 (pb : alk. paper)
  1. Generative grammar. 2. Grammar, Comparative and general— Syntax. 3. Chomsky, Noam. Syntactic structures. I. Depiante, Marcela A. II. Stepanov, Arthur. III. Title. IV. Series: Current studies in linguistics series ; 33.
  P158.L377   2000
  415—dc21   99-39907
                                                              CIP

Contents

Preface   vii

Introduction   1

Chapter 1
Structure and Infinity of Human Language   5

1.1   Structure   5

1.2   Infinity   11

Exercises   34

1.3   English Verbal Morphology   35

Chapter 2
Transformational Grammar   51

2.1   What Is a Transformation?   51

2.2   A First Look at Transformations: The Number and Auxiliary Transformations T15 and T20   53

2.3   Properties of Transformations   56

2.4   Other Properties of Transformations   64

2.5   Transformations in *Syntactic Structures*   66

Exercises   105

2.6   Theoretical Issues Raised by *Syntactic Structures*   106

2.7   Learnability and Language Acquisition   114

Exercises   124

Chapter 3
Verbal Morphology: *Syntactic Structures* and Beyond   125

3.1   Problems in *Syntactic Structures*   125

Contents

3.2   X-Bar Theory   128

3.3   Subcategorization and Selection   129

3.4   English Verbal Morphology Revisited   136

3.5   V-Raising and Split I   163

3.6   Verb Movement and Economy: Chomsky 1991   165

3.7   Chomsky 1993   181

3.8   *Syntactic Structures* Revived: Lasnik 1995   187

Notes   197

References   203

Index   207

Preface

This book is an introduction to some classic ideas and analyses of transformational generative grammar, viewed both on their own terms and from a more modern perspective. Like *A Course in GB Syntax* (Lasnik and Uriagereka 1988), the book grew out of a transcript (created from tapes) of a portion of a course, in particular, the first several units of the first-semester graduate syntax course at the University of Connecticut. The tapes were made in the fall of 1995, and Marcela Depiante, a UConn graduate student, did the transcription and initial editing the following year. Arthur Stepanov, another UConn graduate student, did the subsequent editing, including organizing the material into chapters, numbering the examples, and providing bibliographic references.

In the book, as in the course, I examine in considerable detail the central analyses presented by Noam Chomsky in *Syntactic Structures* (1957) and the theory underlying those analyses, a theory completely formulated in Chomsky's (1955) *The Logical Structure of Linguistic Theory*. The major focus is on the best set of analyses in *Syntactic Structures* and *The Logical Structure of Linguistic Theory* (and, in many respects, the best set of analyses in the history of our field), those treating English verbal morphology. I show how the technology works, often filling in underlying assumptions and formal particulars that are left unstated in *Syntactic Structures*. I emphasize the virtues of these analyses because those virtues have been overlooked in recent decades.

However, as is well known, the analyses are not without defects, particularly with respect to questions of explanatory adequacy, that is, questions of how the child, faced with limited data, arrives at the correct grammar out of the vast set of possible grammars made available by the theory. Thus, in this book, after laying out the *Syntactic Structures* account, I follow the pendulum swing the field took toward greater explanatory adequacy, as I present successive theoretical developments and revisions, both in general and, particularly, as they pertain to treatments of verbal morphology. I explicate Chomsky's first economy-based account, in "Some Notes on Economy of Derivation and Representation" (1991), and then compare it with his minimalist approach in "A Minimalist Program for Linguistic Theory" (1993). The discussion culminates in a presentation of a hybrid theory of English verbal morphology (my "Verbal Morphology: *Syntactic Structures* Meets the Minimalist Program" (1995)), one including elements of both *Syntactic Structures* and "A Minimalist Program for Linguistic Theory."

Chapter 1 presents two of the most fundamental properties of human language: that sentences have structure, and that there are an unlimited number of possible sentences. Early generative theories of these two properties, and of the intimate connection between them, are presented. Finally, the central phenomena of English verbal morphology are introduced and generalizations developed.

Chapter 2 introduces the transformational mechanisms of *Syntactic Structures* and their application to the phenomena presented in chapter 1. The framework behind the transformations is elaborated and examined; some problems, mainly in the realm of explanatory adequacy, are investigated; and directions for solutions are considered. Both chapters 1 and 2 contain exercises on the technical material.

Chapter 3 carries these solutions further, along the way introducing some of the technical developments of Chomsky's *Aspects of the Theory of Syntax* (1965), "Remarks on Nominalization" (1970), and *Barriers* (1986), before arriving at recent economy/minimalist accounts.

I would like to thank Amy Brand and Jay Keyser for their encouragement in this project, and my wife Roberta for her encouragement in all of my endeavors. I am also indebted to the Department of Linguistics at the University of Connecticut for making it possible for me to annually teach my somewhat unconventional introduction to syntax course, of which this book represents a part. Special thanks to Adolfo Ausín and Cédric Boeckx for extensive corrections and suggestions on the previous draft and to Anne Mark, arguably the second most important person in the field, for her usual outstanding editing job. My deepest appreciation goes to the students who have taken the course over the years, especially those who took it in 1995, the year the tapes that turned into this book were made. The students who are quoted in the discussion are Deborah Chen, Marcela Depiante, Edita Gutiérrez, Saša Vukić, and Maki Yamane.

Howard Lasnik

We have been fortunate to attend Howard Lasnik's unique syntax course, which focuses on the ideas and analyses underlying early generative grammar and their relevance in contemporary syntactic theory. We have been even more fortunate to be involved in the project of editing his lectures and putting them together as a book. Our goal was to preserve the overall perspective, as well as those subtle and insightful remarks that characterized this course. It is our hope that students beginning to work in generative syntax and other interested readers will find exploring this book as useful and inspiring as working on it was for us.

For their participation, we would like to thank those who attended the course in the fall of 1995: Dan Blair, Deborah Chen, Edita Gutiérrez, Saša Vukić, and Maki Yamane. Special thanks to Dan Blair for providing us with a good portion of the tapes needed for transcribing the lectures and to Cedric Boeckx for help with the index.

Marcela Depiante
Arthur Stepanov

Introduction

Our concerns in this course will be driven by two fundamental inquiries:

What is "knowledge of language"?
How does it arise in the individual?

At the beginning, I want to forestall some potential confusion that has overtaken a large part of the field. In fact, there are two branches of the investigation of language. One is represented by "practitioners," that is, practicing linguists, practicing psychologists, and so on. The other is the "reflective" part of the field represented by philosophers and cognitive scientists who are concerned with deep conceptual issues relating to the study of language. The confusion has arisen in the "reflective" branch, which often tries to treat natural language words as if they were technical terms and vice versa. Consider the following English sentence:

(1) Howard knows English

Philosophers have always been quite rightly concerned with the concept "knowledge." However, the trap is to think that a sentence like (1) can tell us something about this and other concepts. There is no a priori reason to think that it can. To see the point, consider this:

(2) Howard forced Arthur to leave the room

There is no reason to think that this sentence can tell a physicist something about the concept "force." That seems trivially obvious. (1) is a similar case, but it is actually misleading in two ways. One way in which it is misleading is that it uses the word *know*. However, there are languages (like French) that do not even use the word for *know* in expressing the meaning of (1). The other way in which (1) is misleading is that it looks like a two-place predicate *know* establishing some kind of relation (or "knowing") between *Howard* and *English*. Assuming that individuals like

"Howard" exist, and given this relation of "knowing," the question is, what is this object "English"?

This object has some peculiar properties. One such property is that a sentence like

(3) This floor needs washing

is and is not a part of English. In some parts of the United States, in particular, western Pennsylvania, this sentence is never said (although still understood), whereas in the rest of the country it is perfectly good. Conversely, a sentence like

(4) This floor needs washed

is not and is a part of English, since it is said in the parts of the country where (3) is not acceptable, whereas for people in the rest of the country it sounds very peculiar. It is easy to multiply parallel examples. What is "English," then, the system that has these strange contradictory properties? It is some sort of sociological and political construct, based on things like history and colors on a map. Following standard usage, I will continue to use terms like *English* and *Russian*, but I will be careful not to attribute much significance to them.

Thus, we cannot get too far investigating the concepts we are interested in just by relying on common sense or by looking at sentences of natural language. We want to treat sentences of natural languages as *data* that we need to analyze, but we do not expect them to tell us what the *concepts* of our field are.

Following Chomsky, the approach that I want to take is the following: I will not grant (1) any theoretical significance, and I will be treating the investigation as one of *individual psychology*. I assume that what is characterized as "knowledge of English" is actually some sort of *mental state*, ultimately a state of the brain. Put differently, it is some "arrangement of stuff" in the brain. We are going to try to find out what this "arrangement" is.

One answer to the two questions posed above, popular in the mid 20th century, would say that language is a list of behaviors and that children acquire it by some version of "operant conditioning." This is part of a view of human beings that considers the mind initially like a blank slate, a *tabula rasa*. Of course, no one ever thought that this was literally true. There is a clear difference between a human being and a chair: a chair cannot learn language under any circumstances.

Knowledge of language cannot be a list of behaviors. Linguists came to that conclusion for many reasons, but they can be summed up in the term that Chomsky often uses (borrowed from Humboldt, and perhaps most significantly Descartes): the *creative aspect of language use*. What does this mean? Speakers of human languages can produce and understand sentences they've never heard or produced before. How can a behavior that was never produced before be shaped by operant conditioning? One frequent answer invokes analogy; that is to say, the new behaviors we produce that we haven't produced before are "analogous" to behaviors that we have produced and have been reinforced for before. The hard question is how to make the notion "analogous" precise. Ultimately, the right notion of analogy will have to be something like what can be found in pages 111–114 of *Syntactic Structures*, a set of rules for one kind of *structure* and another set of rules for relating one structure to another. But then, why call it analogy at all?

The list of behaviors of which knowledge of language purportedly consists has to rely on notions like "utterance" and "word." But what is a word? What is an utterance? These notions are already quite abstract. Even more abstract is the notion "sentence." Chomsky has been and continues to be criticized for positing such abstract notions as transformations and structures, but the big leap is what everyone takes for granted. It's widely assumed that the big step is going from sentence to transformation, but this in fact isn't a significant leap. The big step is going from "noise" to "word."

Once we have some notion of structure, we are in a position to address the old question of the creative aspect of language use, and we can begin to deal with the notion of *infinity* (in particular, discrete infinity). The ability to produce and understand new sentences is intuitively related to the notion of infinity. Infinity is one of the most fundamental properties of human languages, maybe the most fundamental one. People debate what the true linguistic universals are, but indisputably, infinity is central.

We need to find a way of representing structure that allows for infinity—in other words, that allows for a sentence inside a sentence inside a sentence, and so on. For example:

(5) John won the race

(6) Mary thinks that John won the race

(7) I regret that Mary thinks that John won the race
    etc.

At some point we will reach a sentence so long that it has never been produced, and will never be produced. At some point we will reach a sentence so long that a human being would die before he or she finished saying it. But that is not a *linguistic* fact.

Contrary to what is sometimes thought about Chomsky's position on these matters, to assume that human languages are infinite is not a *complicating* assumption, but a *simplifying* assumption. As we will see, it is trivial to construct theories of sentence structure that allow an infinite number of sentences, but absurdly cumbersome to construct theories of sentence structure that allow sentences up to, say, 1,000 words long and no longer.

In *Syntactic Structures* Chomsky discussed successively more powerful theories of structure, showing the inadequacy of each. We will retrace those theories very briefly.

I will present this elementary material roughly as Chomsky did in *Syntactic Structures*.[1] Before I do this, however, I want to say a few words about why I'm going to base a large part of the discussion on something that seems so old and outmoded by the standards of current syntactic theorizing. I have three reasons. First, many of the terms, concepts, and analyses in recent work are much easier to understand against a backdrop of their ancestors of a few decades ago. Second, our field is a relatively young one without a large number of good arguments and analyses to use as models. We can't yet afford to ignore some of the good arguments and analyses, even if we conclude that they're ultimately incorrect. Finally, and probably most importantly, I believe that many of the analyses of the 1950s *are* actually correct, fundamentally and (sometimes) even in detail. The discussion will eventually work its way back to this point.

Chapter 1

Structure and Infinity of Human Language

To begin, we want to understand the capabilities and limitations of some primitive theories of language. Our initial criteria will be that a theory of language needs to have some notion of structure and some way of representing infinity—that is, some way of capturing the fact that there is no longest sentence of English or French or any other human language. Let's start by looking at certain elementary structural properties of human languages.

1.1 STRUCTURE

1.1.1 Structure Dependence

Consider the following pairs of sentences, acceptable to native speakers of English:

(1) a. Susan must leave
    b. Must Susan leave?

(2) a. Bill is sleeping
    b. Is Bill sleeping?

There are many interesting facts about these pairs of examples. One is that for sentences like (a) in (1) and (2) there always exist sentences like (b). Another is that the (a) and (b) sentences in both (1) and (2) "feel related" to all English speakers (importantly, to children as well). Assuming that the acceptability of the (a) sentences may be somehow explained, can we explain why the (b) sentences are possible too?

Sometimes it's claimed that the (a) and (b) sentences in (1) and (2) feel related because they "mean the same thing." I've never understood that claim. Even the most trivial semantic theory tells us that (a) and (b) in each of (1) and (2) do *not* mean the same thing. Further, two sentences that *do* mean the same thing typically do not feel related. Consider the following examples:

(3) a. My father's brother purchased an automobile
      b. My uncle bought a car

These examples certainly do not "feel related," although they presumably mean the same thing. On these grounds, at least, it seems pretty obvious that the phenomenon in (1) and (2) can't be grounded on sameness of meaning.

Let's imagine that there's some process involved in "felt-relatedness" of (a) and (b) in (1) and (2) (such that the language-acquiring child's task is to figure out this process). In particular, suppose (substantially oversimplifying) that this process takes the (a) sentences as basic and does something to them, resulting in the (b) sentences. Notice that there's not yet any empirical or any other motivation for taking the (a) sentences as basic. It might turn out that the (b) sentences are basic, or that something else is basic. For now we simply assume that the (a) sentences are basic to get the investigation off the ground. Given that, what might the process be that we're looking for?

Granting, as standardly assumed, the existence of such things as sentences and words, suppose this process is the following:

(4) Invert the first two words in the (a) sentences.

This works well for (1) and (2), and it refers only to sentences and words (surely irreducible) and, perhaps, "counting to 2." But now consider these examples (the star indicates an example that isn't accepted by native speakers of English):

(5) a. Mary read the book
      b. *Read Mary the book?

(6) a. The man left
      b. *Man the left?

Here we applied (4) and got the wrong results, indicating that (4) isn't the correct hypothesis. In order to pose another hypothesis, we'll need more than just words, sentences, and counting to 2. Suppose that we (and the child) distinguish what kinds of words can be involved in the process in question and what kinds can't be. For the moment let's call *must* in (1) and *is* in (2) *auxiliaries* (without adding any substance to this term yet). Our new hypothesis is this:

(7) Move the auxiliary to the front.

This still works for (1) and (2), and now also for (5) and (6) (i.e., it fails to produce the unacceptable (b) cases, since *read* in (5) and *the* in (6) aren't auxiliaries). As good as it is, unfortunately, (7) still isn't good enough. Consider (8).

(8) Mary has been sleeping

Presumably, (8) has two auxiliaries (if *be(en)* is also an auxiliary), but (7) presupposes that the sentence has only one. Changing *the auxiliary* in (7) to *an auxiliary* wouldn't help much, since then (7) would allow an unacceptable counterpart of (8) where the second auxiliary has moved.

(9) *Been Mary has sleeping?

Let's try the following modified hypothesis:

(10) Move the first auxiliary to the front.

This straightforwardly applies to every example that has auxiliaries in it. It seems then to serve as an adequate rule for English "interrogatives." But what about (5a) and (6a), sentences with no auxiliaries at all? One might say that some other process operates there to give a corresponding interrogative sentence. That suggestion isn't ultimately desirable, although for the moment we have to live with it.

   Even apart from this limitation, Chomsky has pointed out a type of example that's problematic for the hypothesis in (10).

(11) The man who is here can swim

(11) has two indisputable auxiliaries, *is* and *can*. If, following (10), we move the first auxiliary to the front, our result is (12).

(12) *Is the man who here can swim?

That's complete gibberish.

   What's particularly interesting is that we have to look pretty far to find cases where hypothesis (10) fails. For the vast majority of sentences, (10) works fine (modulo the additional process needed to deal with sentences like (5a) and (6a), where the desired results are *Did Mary read the book?* and *Did the man leave?*). And cases lacking the complexity of (11)–(12)

are going to be the entirety of the data that children are likely to be exposed to. So we might expect that children would make mistakes like (12) and then get corrected. But no child has ever been documented making these mistakes. Notably, Crain and Nakayama (1987) did relevant experiments involving elicited production of yes-no questions, which clearly demonstrated that children don't make this kind of mistake (which they, following Chomsky, called a *non-structure-dependent error*). This is a remarkable result. Why don't children make these errors? By far, the most plausible answer is that children are designed so as not to be *able* to make them. When a child is hypothesizing what the question-forming processes are, certain hypotheses are available, others aren't. One that isn't available is the type shown in (10): count the words, label them, and do something with them based on counting. By the same token, no language relates interrogative sentences to declaratives by reading the declarative sentence back to front, by inverting the second and fifth words in the declarative, and so on. A priori, there's no reason why this should be the case (one can easily write a computer language that has these properties). But no human language seems to have these properties.

The right description of the process we're talking about will be stated in terms of *structures*, in terms of hierarchical groupings of words, something like (13),

(13) Move the first auxiliary after the subject to the front.

where the subject can be characterized as a word, two words, three words, and so on, or, more generally, some structure that might be indefinitely long. The right rule is thus *structure dependent*, and, on the face of it, vastly more complicated than the wrong rules rejected above. Chomsky has pretty consistently argued over the years that transformational (displacement) processes of human language never count words or do something to such and such a word. Instead, they are structure dependent: they always look at structures and do something with structured representations.

With the rule in (13), we get the right interrogative form of (11).

(14) Can the man who is here swim?

In order to correctly apply (13), we thus need to identify the subject: *the man who is here*. This then is an argument against viewing sentences as just strings of words, and in favor of viewing them as certain hierarchichal groupings of words. We thus need some procedure that provides a *labeled bracketing*. This procedure will "bracket" some words together and then label the group, so we can then identify the bracketed group of words as a subject.

It will turn out that the label is not really going to be "subject." Chomsky (explicitly in *Aspects of the Theory of Syntax* (1965)) rejects this label for the following reason. In (11) *the man who is here* is certainly a subject. But if we introduce the syntactic category "subject," we will miss an overwhelming generalization: *the man who is here* can also be an object, or an object of a preposition, as in the following examples:

(15) a. I saw [the man who is here]
     b. I talked to [the man who is here]

Similarly for *Susan* in (1) or *Bill* in (2) and so on. It would be a huge coincidence that these same bracketings—these same units of structure—can be found in different positions in a sentence. Thus, we do not want "subject" and "object" to be basic notions in our analysis. Instead, we want those bracketings to have the same label (Chomsky used the term *Noun Phrase* (NP)) wherever they can appear—in the position of subject, object, or object of a preposition—thus capturing the generalization.

Many further phenomena confirm the idea that sentences are structured, that the words in them are grouped into *constituents*.

1.1.2 Constituency Tests

1.1.2.1 Pronominalization
Various tests have proved to be useful in determining what groups of words work together as units of structure, or constituents. One such *constituency test* is whether or not elements can be replaced by pronominal forms.

(16) John left

(17) He left

We might conclude from these sentences that "A pronoun stands for a noun," just as the word *pronoun* suggests. But consider the following cases:

(18) The man left

(19) *The he left

(17) He left

Now, from all of (16)–(19) we might conclude that "A pronoun stands for a noun or a noun preceded by *the*." But look at these examples:

(20)   The old man left

(21)   The man in the room left

(22) *He in the room left

(17)   He left

Adding these cases to the previous ones, we once again need to change our conclusion and say that "A pronoun stands for a noun, or a noun preceded by *the*, or a noun preceded by *the* and followed by..."

Clearly, we're missing a generalization. Somehow, we have to say that *John* has something in common with *the man* and with *the man in the room*, and also with *the old man*, *the old old old man*, and so on. Plausibly, there's some higher-level abstract structural unit, such that the kind of position that *John* fills in (16) can be filled by more complicated elements like *the man* or *the old man* or *the old old old man*.

Following tradition, we will say that *John* is an NP (*noun phrase*, an expression somehow based on a noun), *the man* is an NP, *the man in the room* is an NP, *the old man* is an NP, and *he* is an NP. This is pretty abstract, since *NP* is a symbol that has no phonetic manifestation; we don't pronounce it.

1.1.2.2   Topicalization
A second constituency test involves topicalization. Consider the following pair:

(23) I like John

(24) John, I like

Looking at these sentences, we might conjecture that topicalization is a process whereby we "take a noun and move it to the front of the sentence." Now consider (25)–(27).

(25)   I like the man

(26) *Man, I like the

(27)   The man, I like

From these sentences, we see that we need to refine our description of topicalization to the following statement: "Take a noun preceded by a definite article, and move both to the front of the sentence." But now consider these cases:

(28)   I like the old man

(28)   *Man, I like the old

(30)   The old man, I like

Given these examples, we need to refine our statement even further: "Take a noun preceded by an adjective (or by adjectives) and a definite article, and move it to the front of the sentence."

Clearly, we're facing the same type of problem we ran into with pronominalization. How can we characterize the portion of the sentence that undergoes topicalization? It's not just *John*; it's not just *the man*; it's not just *the old man*; it's not just *the old old man*; and so on. It seems, then, that we need a more abstract notion of structure that says that *John*, *the man*, and *the old old man* are the same type of unit.

1.1.2.3   Coordination

A third constituency test involves coordination. Consider the following examples:

(31)   I like John and the man

(32)   I like John and the old man

(33)   *I like John and to go to the movies
         (cf. I like John; I like to go to the movies)

Generally speaking (as the ungrammaticality of trying to coordinate *John* and *to go to the movies* shows), only elements of the same type can be coordinated. Therefore, *John*, *the man*, and *the old man* must be of the same type. Why should they be behaving like elements of the same type? How can we characterize this other than in terms of a structural unit?

1.2   INFINITY

Earlier we excluded the possibility that the right answer to the question "What is 'knowledge of language'?" could be "Some kind of a list." Why is that? Because we're dealing with individual psychology, and if the answer to the question is "Some kind of a list," then we are saying that that list is in the human brain. If we go on to say that the set of potential behaviors we're interested in characterizing is infinite, then we're saying that there's an infinitely long list in the brain. But how can there be an infinitely long list in the brain? The brain is finite; it's big, but it's finite. So, the simplest formal device that Chomsky was willing to discuss to answer the question "What is 'knowledge of language'?" is the simplest one that can capture infinity. It's called a *finite-state machine/device* (see chapter 3 in *Syntactic Structures*).

1.2.1 Finite-State Grammars

A finite-state device (or *Markov process*) consists of

- An initial state
- A finite number of states
- A specification of transitions from one state to another (not necessarily distinct)
- A specification of a symbol (or a finite number of symbols) that will be printed when a particular transition obtains
- A final state

Let's look at the simple finite-state machine in (34) (equivalent to (7) on page 19 of *Syntactic Structures*). The circles in (34) represent the five states of the machine. The arrows represent transitions from state to state. ① is designated as the initial state and ④ as the final state. The words above the arrows are the symbols that are printed when a particular transition obtains. So, in (34), upon the transition from the first state to the second state, the symbol *The* is printed.

(34)

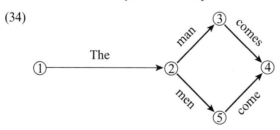

The finite-state grammar in (34) is the representation of a language consisting of only two sentences: *The man comes* and *The men come*.

Recall that we're interested in infinity. Is there any way that we can characterize infinity with a finite-state device? Let's look at the finite-state grammar in (35) (equivalent to (8) on page 19 of *Syntactic Structures*).

(35)

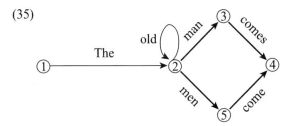

The grammar in (35) generates the same sentences that the grammar in (34) generated. But it can also generate *The old old man/men . . .* and *The old old old man/men. . . .* We can indeed capture infinity with this machine.

For exposition, and sticking to *Syntactic Structures* terminology, we're temporarily taking a language to be a set of sentences. We're taking a grammar to be a formal machine for generating sentences. A derivation is a sequence of formal computations that results in a sentence (string of symbols).

Let's look at how a finite-state machine will generate a sentence like the following:

(36) The man runs and runs and runs and runs

A machine that generates (36) is shown in (37).

(37)

In addition to (36), the grammar in (37) can generate the following sentences:

(38) The man runs

(39) The man runs and runs

(40) The man runs and runs and runs

The finite-state device in (37) also captures infinity.

1.2.2   Limitations of Finite-State Devices

It's possible to construct some purely formal language and ask whether it's a finite-state language or not. That's what Chomsky does in *Syntactic Structures* (page 21).

Let's look at some formal languages that aren't finite-state languages ((10i) in *Syntactic Structures*). Consider the sentences of the language in (41).

(41) ab
      aabb
      aaabbb
      aaaabbbb

      . . .

This language can be characterized as consisting of sentences with any number of a's followed by exactly the same number of b's as long as that number is greater than 0 ($a^n b^n$, $n > 0$, using a fairly standard notation).

Can we construct a finite-state grammar for the language in (41)? Let's see if (42) captures this language, whose sentences always contain equal numbers of a's and b's.

(42)

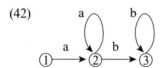

The language that the grammar in (42) can generate is $a^n b^m$, that is, any number of a's followed by any number of b's; but this is different from the language in (41) that we were trying to generate, where a certain number of a's are followed by *exactly the same* number of b's.

The finite-state grammar in (42) *overgenerates*. It can generate all of the sentences of the language in (41), but it also generates many more sentences that aren't part of the language. There's no way to connect up the number of a's with the number of b's. Because (42) has a loop on a, it can generate an unbounded number of a's, and because it has a loop on b, it can generate an unbounded number of b's; but neither loop can "see" the other loop.

This is exactly what it means for a machine to be a finite-state machine. When it's in a particular state, all it knows is what state it's in, what state it can get to from there, and what symbol it will be printing. It doesn't know what state it used to be in or how many times it's been in that state. The limitation of finite-state machines is that they have no memory—precisely the limitation that prevents them from successfully characterizing the language in (41).

Let's look now at Chomsky's second example, the formal language in (43), called a *mirror-image language* ((10ii) in *Syntactic Structures*).

(43) aa
     bb
     abba
     baab
     abbbba
     . . .

Let's see if we can construct a finite-state machine to generate this language. First, let's try to generate the first part of the sentences in (43). In other words, can we write a finite-state machine to generate any number of *a*'s and *b*'s in any order?

(44) a

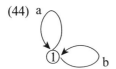

With the finite-state machine in (44) we can indeed generate any number of *a*'s and any number of *b*'s in any order. But now to generate (43) we also have to be able to generate the mirror image of the sentences that we've generated with the grammar in (44). We can't do this with a finite-state grammar, however, because as we just saw, finite-state machines have no memory.

There's also a human language analogue to the formal languages mentioned above. This example (which I got from Morris Halle, my first linguistics teacher) comes from the realm of word compounding. The military arsenals of many countries have *missiles*. They may also have so-called *anti-missile missiles*, designed to shoot an enemy missile out of the sky. Now, in order to neutralize the anti-missile missiles, the enemy may create something called *anti-anti-missile missile missiles*. There are presumably technological limits on how far one can go in creating this kind of weapon, but there are no linguistic limits as far as the corresponding word formation process is concerned. Let's notate the situation as follows:

(45) anti^n missile^{n+1}
     (*n anti*'s followed by *n* + 1 *missile*'s)

As in the case of the formal languages considered above, we can't characterize this language with a finite-state grammar, and for the same reason: such a grammar can't keep track of the number of *anti*'s in order to make the number of *missile*'s greater by one.

Finite-state devices have other limitations, as well. Recall that we had proposed the following rule for forming yes-no questions in English:

(13) Move the first auxiliary after the subject to the front.

We've seen that there seems to be no limit on how long the subject of a sentence can be. There's no clear way of characterizing the notion "subject" in terms of number of words. Instead, we have to characterize it with some notion of *structure*. We have to say that *the*, *old*, and *man* in (20), for example, go together and make up some kind of unit. And so far the finite-state device can't capture this. For finite-state machines, sentences are just strings of symbols that get printed on the transitions. This is an obvious limitation of finite-state devices.

Finite-state devices allow us to generate sentences by printing out symbols sequentially but don't determine any abstract structure. We need a more abstract theory that allows us to characterize structure, that allows us to say that words aren't just pearls on a string but entities that can be grouped in natural ways.

It turns out that there's no way to characterize languages like (41) and (43) without introducing abstract structure. Such languages are said to have *unbounded discontinuous dependencies*. The presence of one symbol depends on the presence of another that's an arbitrary distance away in the string, a state of affairs that's beyond the bounds of finite-state description. To overcome this fundamental limitation of finite-state grammars, we will turn to a less elementary, more powerful model that will allow us to describe the languages in (41) and (43) and that will automatically determine abstract structure: phrase structure grammar.

1.2.3   Phrase Structure Grammars

We need a system that allows us to introduce two symbols at the same time, such that these symbols aren't necessarily adjacent to each other. For example, for the "mirror-image language" (43) we need to ensure that when we introduce an *a* at the beginning of a sentence, we're also introducing an *a* at the end of that sentence. We'll see that *context-free* phrase structure (PS) grammars have that power, and with them we can generate languages (41) and (43).

Context-free PS grammars (or *[Σ, F] grammars* in Chomsky's terminology) consist of

- A designated initial symbol (Σ)
- Rewrite rules (F), which consist of one symbol on the left, followed by an arrow, followed by at least one symbol

A PS rule like (46b) will allow us to introduce the symbol *a* at the beginning of a sentence and *at the same time* introduce the symbol *b* at the end of the sentence. The rule allows us to introduce these two symbols simultaneously, without their being adjacent to each other.

(46) a. Σ: S
     b. F: S → aSb

Here is what the symbols in (46) stand for:

S   designated initial symbol; also, an abstract, nonterminal symbol that will not be part of any sentence (nonterminal symbols are those that appear on the left side of rewrite rules—hence, are rewritten)

→   a symbol meaning 'rewrite as' or 'consists of'

a, b   terminal symbols (i.e., those that are not "rewritten"—hence, appear in the output sentence)

In contrast, the rewrite rules in a *context-sensitive PS grammar* consist of

- A single symbol on the left
- An arrow
- One or more terminal or nonterminal symbols
- A specification of the circumstances under which the rewriting takes place

For example:

(47) c → d/e ____ f
     (or, in other words: ecf → edf)

Many phonological rules in Chomsky and Halle 1968 are context-sensitive rewrite rules. For our purposes right now, however, we will be mainly concerned with rules of the context-free type.

We also need a (recursive) definition of a *derivation*. A derivation consists of a series of lines such that the first line is the designated initial symbol, and the procedure for moving from one line to the next is to replace exactly one symbol by the sequence of symbols it can be rewritten as.

For example, the portion of a PS grammar in (46b) will generate a portion of a derivation that looks like this:

(48) Line 1:   S
     Line 2:   aSb
     Line 3:   aaSbb
     Line 4:   aaaSbbb

Notice that no matter how many times we reapply (46b), the resulting string still contains a nonterminal symbol. In order to "turn off the machine" and end the derivation, we must add one more rule:

(49) S → ab

With rule (49) we can rewrite S as *ab* and end the derivation with line (5):

(48) Line 5:   aaaabbbb

Thus, the PS grammar incorporating rules (46) and (49) generates the language in (41).

PS grammars allow us to pair up two symbols no matter how much "stuff" is in between. Why? Because the two symbols were introduced by the same application of the same rewrite rule.

The fundamental descriptive advantage of PS grammars compared with finite-state grammars is that PS grammars can pair up elements that are indefinitely far apart. They do this by introducing symbols that are never physically manifested: the nonterminal symbols. We can't turn off the machine until we get rid of all nonterminal symbols. Nonterminal symbols are what we will use to characterize the notion of structure we were concerned about earlier. Why does *John* behave like *the man*, and why does *sleep* behave like *solve the problem*? It's because with respect to the symbols that don't get pronounced (nonterminal symbols), they're the same, even though with respect to the symbols that do get pronounced (terminal symbols), they're wildly different.

We'll look now in detail at how PS grammars represent structure and concentrate on a precise way of doing it.

Let's look at an example of a PS grammar that more closely (though still pretty abstractly) characterizes human language.

(50) a. Designated initial symbol: S
     b. Rewrite rules (F):
        S → NP VP
        NP → N
        VP → V
        N → John
        N → Mary
        V → laughs
        V → sings
        V → thinks

In this grammar the nonterminal symbols (symbols that can be rewritten) are S, NP, VP, V, N;[1] the terminal symbols (symbols that can't be rewritten) are *John, Mary, laughs, sings*.

Here's an example of a derivation using the PS grammar (50):

(51) Line 1:   S
    Line 2:   NP VP
    Line 3:   N VP[2]
    Line 4:   N V
    Line 5:   Mary V
    Line 6:   Mary laughs
    = STOP =

Let's not forget that we need to capture infinity. The PS rules in our little model grammar don't do so. Let's then introduce the following rule (anachronistically, since the *Syntactic Structures* model actually didn't have this type of "recursive" PS rule):

(52) VP → V S

Rule (52) is analogous to a loop in the finite-state grammar (recall, e.g., (35) and (37)). It is the "cost" of infinity, which is, in fact, very cheap. Adding rule (52) allows us to generate an infinite number of sentences of the following type:

(53) a. John thinks Mary sings/laughs
    b. John thinks Mary thinks John sings/laughs
    c. John thinks Mary thinks John thinks Mary sings/laughs
       etc.

Thus, by introducing a rule such as (52), which allows us to generate a sentence inside another sentence, we have captured infinity.

Let's now look at one of the many equivalent derivations of one of the sentences in (53), namely, (53a).

(53) a. John thinks Mary sings

(54) Line 1:   S
    Line 2:   NP VP
    Line 3:   N VP
    Line 4:   N V S[3]
    Line 5:   N V NP VP
    Line 6:   N V N VP
    Line 7:   N V N V

Line 8:   John V N V
Line 9:   John thinks N V
Line 10:   John thinks Mary V
Line 11:   John thinks Mary sings
= STOP =

These rules also generate the following sentences:

(55) Mary thinks John laughs

(56) Mary thinks John sings

However, they generate the following unacceptable ones as well:

(57) *John sings Mary laughs

(58) *John laughs John sings

(59) *John laughs Mary sings

That is, our PS grammar is overgenerating. It's able to generate sentences that aren't part of the English language. The sentences are "English-like" (in word order and structure), but aren't acceptable. Eventually we will address this apparent inadequacy of the model.

PS grammars capture constituent structure by introducing nonterminal symbols. Recall earlier arguments where we concluded that at some level of abstraction *the man*, *the old man*, and *the old old man* all have to be the same type of element. PS grammars allow us to group these phrases under the same nonterminal symbol, NP.

Suppose we take (61), which is one derivation for (60), produced by the grammar introduced in (50) and (52).

(60) John thinks Mary sings

(61) Line 1:   S
     Line 2:   NP VP
     Line 3:   N VP
     Line 4:   N V S
     Line 5:   N V NP VP
     Line 6:   N V N VP
     Line 7:   N V N V
     Line 8:   John V N V
     Line 9:   John thinks N V
     Line 10:   John thinks Mary V
     Line 11:   John thinks Mary sings

We now connect each symbol with the symbols it was rewritten as. In this way we represent the derivation in the form of a *PS tree*, shown in (62), and we can trace back units of structure.

(62)

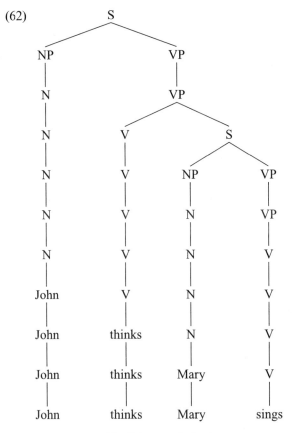

Now we can get rid of the symbols that are mere repetitions. In this way, we end up with (63), which is called a *collapsed PS tree*.[4]

(63)

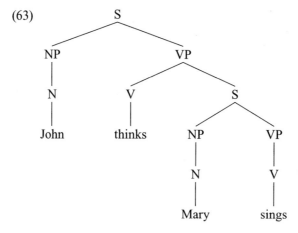

Representing a derivation in this graph-theoretical manner implies a mathematical claim: namely, that no matter which choices we make when we're deriving a terminal string, we will end up with the same collapsed PS tree (abstracting away from structural ambiguity; see below).

To see this point, let's derive the same sentence in a different way and confirm that we get the same collapsed PS tree.

(64) Line 1:   S
      Line 2:   NP VP
      Line 3:   NP V S[5]
      Line 4:   N V S
      Line 5:   N V NP VP
      Line 6:   N V N VP
      Line 7:   N V N V
      Line 8:   John V N V
      Line 9:   John thinks N V
      Line 10:   John thinks Mary V
      Line 11:   John thinks Mary sings

Indeed, the resulting collapsed PS tree (65) is the same as (63).

(65)

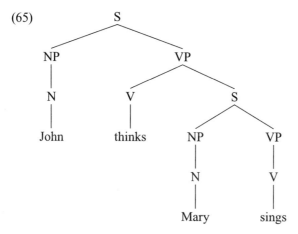

(61) and (64) are two different derivations, but they are in a crucial sense "equivalent." In producing them, we applied the same rules but not in the same *order*. More generally, two PS derivations are equivalent if and only if they involve the same rules, applied the same number of times, but not necessarily in the same order. Recall that we looked at a mechanical algorithm for collapsing a PS derivation down to a PS tree. Indeed, in *The Logical Structure of Linguistic Theory* (1955) Chomsky proved that two PS derivations are equivalent if and only if they collapse down to the same PS tree.

1.2.4 A Note on Recursion

Infinity and structure are arguably the two most fundamental characteristics of human language. We first used finite-state machines to capture infinity; we then changed to PS grammar, a more powerful device that captures both infinity and structure.

At this point I have to admit that (as I hinted earlier) I've been misleading you about one aspect of the theory. Remember Chomsky's formal language arguments for PS grammar. On pretty much that model, I've been analyzing a structure like *John thinks Mary sings* as involving *recursive* PS rules. Rather ironically, however, the theory in both *Syntactic Structures* and *The Logical Structure of Linguistic Theory* (Chomsky 1955; henceforth *LSLT*) didn't have recursion "in the base." Instead, complicated structures were created by special operations, called *generalized transformations*, which put together simpler structures. For example, to derive *John knew that Mary understood the theory*, first the separate structures underlying *John knew it* and *Mary understood the theory* were

generated; then a generalized transformation inserted the second of these
structures into the first. In other words, in this theory recursion was in the
"transformational component." Chomsky listed a few generalized transformations as (22)–(26) on pages 113–114 of *Syntactic Structures*. I will
return to this issue and to arguments surrounding recursion in the base
versus generalized transformations.

1.2.5   Equivalent versus Nonequivalent Derivations

Consider a vaguely human language–type situation involving equivalent
PS derivations and then a vaguely human language–type situation
involving nonequivalent PS derivations.

Suppose we have the following grammar, a fragment of one we looked
at earlier, where V_N and V_T stand for vocabularies of nonterminal and
terminal symbols, respectively:

(66) Σ: S
     F: S → NP VP
             NP → N
             VP → V
             N → John
             V → left
             V_N = {S, NP, VP, N, V}
             V_T = {John, left}

One derivation for *John left* is the following:

(67) Line 1:   S
     Line 2:   NP VP
     Line 3:   N VP
     Line 4:   N V
     Line 5:   John V
     Line 6:   John left

Another derivation for *John left* is the following:

(68) Line 1:   S
     Line 2:   NP VP
     Line 3:   NP V
     Line 4:   N V
     Line 5:   N left
     Line 6:   John left

It's easy to verify that the collapsed PS trees corresponding to these two derivations will be the same.

(69)

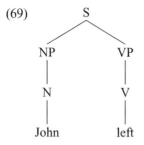

In addition to what we now know about equivalence of derivations, there's also a clear intuitive sense in which the derivations are equivalent. They're telling us the same information about the constituent structure of the sentence. In particular, (69) contains the following information:

(70) *John left* is an S
     John is an N
     John is an NP
     left is a V
     left is a VP

And that's arguably everything there is to know about the structure of this sentence.

Similarly, from the tree in (63)/(65) we can conclude the following information:

(71) *Mary* is an N and an NP
     sings is a V and a VP
     Mary sings is an S
     thinks Mary sings is a VP
     John is an N and an NP
     John thinks Mary sings is an S

This kind of information is represented as what Chomsky called in *Syntactic Structures "is a"* relations. We needn't worry about the details of this notion at this point. In the next section I'll give an algorithm for determining "is a" relations and discuss its importance for the theory.

Now let's look at a more complicated grammar that allows for *nonequivalent* derivations. Nonequivalent derivations are standardly referred to as exhibiting *structural ambiguity*. Chomsky's classic case of structural ambiguity is (72).

(72) Flying planes can be dangerous

I'll use a slightly simpler example right now.

(73) John hit the man with a stick

Suppose we have the grammar in (74) (as usual, not necessarily an actual fragment of the grammar of English). (In this grammar PP = prepositional phrase, P = preposition, Det = determiner.)

(74) Σ: S
      F: S → NP VP
              VP → V NP
              VP → V NP PP
              NP → N
              NP → Det N
              NP → Det N PP
              PP → P NP
              Det → a
              Det → the
              N → John
              N → man
              N → stick
              V → hit
              P → with

In *Aspects of the Theory of Syntax* (Chomsky 1965; henceforth *Aspects*), Chomsky called rules like the last seven rules in (74), which rewrite a particular nonterminal symbol as a single terminal symbol, *lexical insertion rules*. In *Syntactic Structures* he made no such distinction among types of PS rules; this lack of distinction severely limited this model's descriptive power, as we'll see later on.

Let's look at two *nonequivalent* derivations of (73). The first is shown in (75).

(75) Line 1:   S
      Line 2:   NP VP
      Line 3:   N VP
      Line 4:   N V NP PP
      Line 5:   N V NP P NP
      Line 6:   N V Det N P NP
      Line 7:   N V Det N P Det N

Line 8:   N V Det N P a N
Line 9:   John V Det N P a N
Line 10:   John hit Det N P a N
Line 11:   John hit the N P a N
Line 12:   John hit the N with a N
Line 13:   John hit the man with a N
Line 14:   John hit the man with a stick

The collapsed PS tree of this derivation is (76).[6]

(76)

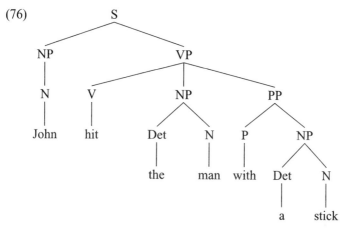

A second derivation and the corresponding PS tree are shown in (77) and (78).

(77) Line 1:   S
     Line 2:   NP VP
     Line 3:   NP V NP
     Line 4:   NP V Det N PP
     Line 5:   N V Det N PP
     Line 6:   N V Det N P NP
     Line 7:   John V Det N P NP
     Line 8:   John hit Det N P NP
     Line 9:   John hit Det N P Det N
     Line 10: John hit the N P Det N
     Line 11: John hit the man P Det N
     Line 12: John hit the man with Det N
     Line 13: John hit the man with a N
     Line 14: John hit the man with a stick

(78)

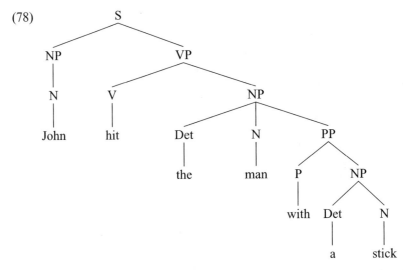

We've generated the sentence we were trying to generate, and we've generated it from the same [Σ, F] grammar we used before. Significantly, though, the derivations (75) and (77) aren't equivalent, because they involve not just a different order of PS rules, but different PS rules. The effect of using different PS rules becomes clear when we collapse the derivations into PS trees ((76) for derivation (75) and (78) for derivation (77)): these two PS trees are different.

Look at what the two different trees (76) and (78) say about the sentence. They both say that *John hit a man with a stick* is an S, that *John* is an N, and that *John* is an NP. They both say that *hit the man with a stick* is a VP, but now they begin to diverge. PS tree (78) says that *the man with a stick* is an NP; however, PS tree (76) says that *the man* is an NP but not that *the man with a stick* is an NP. Let's use two of our constituent structure tests (see section 1.1.2) to see the difference between the interpretations of (76) and (78).[7]

(79) a. John hit the man with a stick (under the interpretation in (78))
      b. John hit him

(80) a. John hit the man with a stick (under the interpretation in (76))
      b. John hit him with a stick

(81) The man with a stick, John hit (has to be the interpretation in (78))

■ *Vukić:*   Let's say we have a PS grammar with the following rules:

(82) S → NP VP

    NP → NP PP

    VP → PP VP

Would that introduce an ambiguity? Look at line 3 of (83a) and (83b)—
PP VP could be connected to VP, or NP PP to NP (see the corresponding
trees in (84)).

(83) a. Line 1: S   b. Line 1: S

         Line 2: NP VP   Line 2: NP VP

         Line 3: NP PP VP   Line 3: NP PP VP

(84) a.   S   b.   S

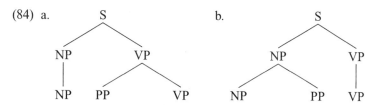

Lasnik: Yes, in principle we can construct such ambiguous cases. This is
potentially a problem, since two clearly different derivations can apparently yield the same sequence of lines. One possible answer to this is to
construct the tree "on-line." That is, we don't wait until we're done with
the whole derivation to construct the tree. Rather, as we proceed from
one line to the next, we make the relevant connections.   ■

1.2.6   Phrase Markers

1.2.6.1   "Is a" Relations

Recall that Chomsky's theory we are considering is based on

- [Σ, F] grammars (context-free PS grammars)
- Derivations
- Equivalence classes of such derivations
- Set theory

Here is Chomsky's set-theoretic formalization of phrase structure (see
Syntactic Structures, pp. 27–29, 87):

(85) Given a particular [Σ, F] grammar and a particular terminal string
      (i.e., string of terminal symbols):

a. Construct all of the equivalent PS derivations of the terminal string.

b. Collect all of the lines occurring in any of those equivalent derivations into a set. This set is the *phrase marker* (PM), a complete representation of the PS of the terminal string.

What do we want a PM to do for us? We want to know for each portion of the terminal string whether that portion comprises a constituent or not, and, when it comprises a constituent, what the "name" of that constituent is.

This theory has an algorithm such that when we apply it, we know exactly the constituent structure of the terminal string and the labeling of the constituents. Specifically, this is an algorithm for determining "is a" relations. (In section 1.2.6.2 we will also discuss a way of simplifying this theory.)

Here is Chomsky's empirical claim: All and only what we want a PM to do is to tell us the "is a" relations between portions of the terminal strings and nonterminal symbols. Anything that tells us those and only those is a perfectly adequate PM; anything that doesn't is inadequate as a PM.

We'll go through an example and see that the resulting PM has some superfluous elements, some things we don't really need. Again, all we need is to determine the "is a" relations. We might build the PM the way we've been doing so far and knock out the excess; the other way is to build it from scratch (Lasnik and Kupin (1977) took the latter course, the simplification I alluded to a moment ago).

Consider the following PS grammar:

(86) Σ: S
     F: S → NP VP
           NP → he
           VP → V
           V → left

Now let's construct all the equivalent derivations for the sentence *He left*.

(87) a. *Derivation 1*
        Line 1:   S
        Line 2:   NP VP
        Line 3:   he VP
        Line 4:   he V
        Line 5:   he left

b. *Derivation 2*
  Line 1:   S
  Line 2:   NP VP
  Line 3:   NP V
  Line 4:   he V
  Line 5:   he left
c. *Derivation 3*
  Line 1:   S
  Line 2:   NP VP
  Line 3:   NP V
  Line 4:   NP left
  Line 5:   he left

The next step is to collect all the lines occurring in any of these equivalent derivations into a set. That set will be the PM (the PS representation of the terminal string *He left*). Here is our resulting PM:

(88) PM = {S̲, he left, he VP̲, he V̲, NP left̲, NP VP, NP V}

Now the question is, looking at the set above, how can we determine what the "is a" relations are? Some members of the set have exactly one nonterminal symbol and any number of terminal symbols. Let's call them *monostrings* (they're underlined in (88)). By comparing the monostrings with the terminal string one by one, we can compute all the "is a" relations as follows. We start by comparing *he left* with *he VP*.

(89) he left
      he VP

From (89), we can deduce that *left* is a VP. Next we compare *he left* with *he V*.

(90) he left
      he V

From (90), we determine that *left* is a V. Next we compare *he left* with *NP left*.

(91) he left
      NP left

From (91), we conclude that *he* is an NP. Finally we compare *he left* with *S*.

(92) he left
    S

From (92), we determine that *he left* is an S.

   Does that tell us everything we want to know about the "is a" relations in this sentence? Let's look at the tree for *He left*, (93), and see what it tells us about the "is a" relations. We know how to get the tree. We just pick one of the equivalent derivations and collapse it.

(93)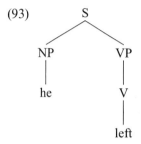

This tree indeed tells us what we've just established.

(94) *he left* is an S
    left is a VP
    left is a V
    he is an NP

   These are all of the "is a" relations involving the terminal string *he left*. According to Chomsky, an adequate theory of PS is a representation of all and only the "is a" relations that hold in a particular sentence, given a particular $[\Sigma, F]$ grammar—that is, a representation of what portions of the terminal string bear the "is a" relations to what nonterminal symbols.

■ *Gutiérrez:*   We also have VP left in the tree.

V

Lasnik: According to Chomsky, we want the theory of PS to tell us the "is a" relations, where the "is a" relations are defined as relations between portions of the terminal string and nonterminal symbols. The tree we just looked at in (93) actually encodes a bit of information beyond the "is a" relations. The extra information, as you point out, is that this VP was rewritten as V, and the V was rewritten as *left*. Now let's look again at (93), alongside another PS tree, (95).

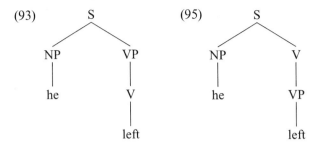

The two graphs (93) and (95) in the graph-theoretic version of PS will collapse into the same set in the set-theoretic representation. Why is that? Because *he V* will be a line in some of the derivations, and *he VP* will be a line in some of the derivations; but the PM is a set, an unordered thing, so there's no way to say that *he VP* comes before *he V*. That's incoherent.

Thus, the graph-theoretic representations encode some information beyond the "is a" relations. The empirical question is, do we need that additional information, say, for phonological, semantic, or further syntactic operations? If we do, then we reject the set-theoretic model; if we don't, then we accept the set-theoretic model, since we would like the minimal theory that does what has to be done. Keep that empirical question in mind as we proceed.   ∎

We've seen up to now that a PM is a representation of the constituent structure of a sentence. For pedagogical reasons, standard presentations of PMs are never set-theoretic; they're always graph-theoretic. A tree on a blackboard is a much more transparent presentation of structure than a set. But in this theory PMs aren't really graph-theoretic.

1.2.6.2 Reduced Phrase Markers

If all we're trying to do is what Chomsky was trying to do (i.e., determine all and only the "is a" relations), then we have a straightforward algorithm for doing that: namely, look at the terminal string and the monostrings. But in general, a set-theoretic PM will contain much more than the terminal strings and the monostrings. Typically, the monostrings constitute a tiny percentage of all of the strings in the PM.

The question is whether we need all this "extra stuff" or not. Lasnik and Kupin (1977) argued that we don't. Since to determine the "is a" relations we only need the terminal strings and the monostrings, Lasnik and Kupin proposed a construct called a *reduced phrase marker* (RPM), which includes only the terminal strings and the monostrings.

In order to construct an RPM, we could construct a PM in Chomsky's sense and then "knock out" everything except the terminal strings and the monostrings. But Lasnik and Kupin didn't do it this way. Instead, they built RPMs from scratch. They asked, what is a PM in a set-theoretic sense? It's a set of strings. So why don't we start by saying that any set of strings is an RPM, but with some conditions imposed on it. Lasnik and Kupin formalized these conditions: a completeness condition, a consistency condition, and so on. That worked out pretty well and it seemed operationally simpler.

In this model it wasn't necessary to go through all the equivalent derivations to get to the PM. Kupin and I actually worried about that at the time. Here was a theory of PS, but it wasn't based on PS rules at all, totally unlike the classic theory. The job of PS rules is to construct equivalent derivations, but this theory didn't need those equivalent derivations. So the question was, does it make sense to have a theory of phrase structure without PS rules? A few years later a very nice answer emerged, most explicitly in Stowell 1981, where it was argued that PS rules are redundant, duplicating information that must be available in other ways regardless. There's some discussion of this in chapter 1 of Lasnik and Uriagereka 1988.

Exercises

1. Present a finite-state grammar, in graphic form, for each of the following languages:

a. My sister laughed
   My sister laughed and laughed
   My sister laughed and laughed and laughed
   etc.

b. Mary saw three old men
   Mary saw three very old men
   Mary saw three very very old men
   Mary saw three very very very old men
   etc.

2. Provide a PS grammar that generates the "mirror-image language" in (43). How many PS rules are necessary and sufficient for this grammar?

3. Given the following context-free PS grammar, give derivations for the sentences *ab*, *aaab*, *aabbbbb*.

S → AB
A → aA

$A \rightarrow a$
$B \rightarrow bB$
$B \rightarrow b$

4. Consider the following PS grammar and provide the information requested in A–C.

$S \rightarrow AB$
$A \rightarrow Aa$
$B \rightarrow b$
$A \rightarrow a$

A. Provide all of the equivalent derivations for the sentence *aab*.
B. Give the set phrase marker for the sentence *aab*.
C. Give the reduced phrase marker for the sentence *aab* (that is, the phrase marker consisting of the terminal string and the monostrings).

[Remember that in getting from one line of a derivation to the next, exactly one rule applies once. Also, recall that two derivations are equivalent if they differ only in the order of application of rules.]

5. Consider the following languages and provide the information requested in A and B.

a. $a^n b c^n$ (*abc*, *aabcc*, *aaabccc*, etc.)
   where n is greater than 0 ($n > 0$)

b. $b^{n+1} a^n$ (*bba*, *bbbaa*, etc.)
   $n > 0$

A. Write context-free grammars for each of these languages. (Make the grammars as simple as possible.)
B. Give derivations for two sentences from each of the languages.

1.3   ENGLISH VERBAL MORPHOLOGY

With this much formal background, let's go through some of the English phenomena that Chomsky brilliantly examined in *Syntactic Structures*. We'll begin by looking at a set of complicated facts quite superficially.

1.3.1   English Auxiliaries

In English a sentence can have a main verb and no "auxiliary verb," as in (96).

(96) John sang

A sentence can also have one auxiliary verb, as in (97).

(97) a. John may sing
     b. John has sung

   c. John will sing

   d. John is singing

   e. John can sing

   f. John could sing

These might be divided into two groups. One group is the following:

(98) a. John may sing

      b. John will sing

      c. John can sing

      d. John could sing

The main verb occurs in its bare form in (98). The second group is the following:

(99) a. John has sung

      b. John is singing

The main verb does not occur in its bare form in (99). Other cases in the same group as (99a) and (99b) are these:

(100) a. John had sung

       b. John was singing

We'll temporarily ignore the differences in the cases above and analyze all of them as forms of *sing*, which collectively we'll call SING (allomorphs of *sing*).

    Now consider the modal auxiliaries. Intuitively, they too are some sort of "helping verb." Syntactically, they all can participate in interrogative inversion: *Must John sing?*, *Could John sing?*, and so on. All of them share the interesting property that when they're followed by the main verb, the main verb is always in its bare form.

    Here's a list of modal auxiliaries in English:

(101) may

      might

      will

      would

      can

      could

      must

      shall

      should

English also has the auxiliary category HAVE, which can take any of the following forms:

(102) has/had/have

And it has the auxiliary category BE, which can take any of the following forms:

(103) am/is/are/was/were

Some sentences have two auxiliary verbs, and in those cases additional forms emerge.

(104) a. John has been singing
       b. John could have sung
       c. John must be singing
       d. John will be singing

A sentence can even have three auxiliary verbs.

(105) John could have been singing

We now have plenty of data. Let's start by formulating some generalizations about auxiliaries; then we'll see how we can formalize those generalizations.

Here's one generalization:

(106) When a sentence contains a modal auxiliary (M), it is always the first thing after the subject.

Here's another:

(107) When HAVE and BE cooccur, BE immediately follows HAVE.

That this is indeed so can be seen from the following examples:

(108) a. John has been singing
       b. John had been singing
       c. John could have been singing

(We hold constant the fact that there will always be a "main" verb.)

Taking modals and HAVE/BE to constitute a natural class of auxiliaries, we notice the ordering information in (109)–(111).

(109) *Cases with one auxiliary*
       M (can occur alone)
       HAVE (can occur alone)
       BE (can occur alone)

(110) *Cases with two auxiliaries*
    a. HAVE BE
       M BE
       M HAVE
    b. *BE HAVE
       *BE M
       *HAVE M
    c. *HAVE HAVE
       *BE BE
       *M M

(111) *Cases with three auxiliaries*
    M HAVE BE

To capture the desired generalization regarding modals and auxiliaries, let's represent a sentence as consisting of the following three parts:

(112) Subject | Aux | Main Verb

That is, we'll say that there's an auxiliary position *Aux*.[8] What can appear in Aux? The following PS rules, in accord with our observations, say that Aux can contain any of the elements shown:

(113) Aux → M
     Aux → HAVE
     Aux → BE
     Aux → M HAVE
     Aux → M BE
     Aux → HAVE BE
     Aux → M HAVE BE

That doesn't look like a generalization at all. Counting the case where there is no apparent auxiliary, there are eight cases and eight rules. What could be worse? How can we possibly make a generalization? Chomsky's proposal in this respect might seem trivial, but it's actually very deep. To fully appreciate it, we need to look at some intellectual background that wasn't made explicit until several years later in *Aspects*.

Throughout his career Chomsky has been concerned with the major questions we're concerned with here: What is our knowledge of language? Where does it come from? How does this knowledge get into our heads? The first question, regarding the nature of linguistic knowledge, Chomsky characterizes in terms of *descriptive adequacy*. A theory of language attains descriptive adequacy if it provides grammars that truly describe the facts of each language. How this linguistic knowledge gets into the head is the question of *explanatory adequacy*. A theory of language attains explanatory adequacy if it provides a procedure by which the learner selects the right grammar on the basis of primary linguistic data (the utterances an infant is exposed to).

In *Aspects* Chomsky proposed a rather precise (if still programmatic) answer to the question of explanatory adequacy. He suggested that certain information is "wired in" the human brain. This information includes the following definitions:

- Definition of a *possible syntactic rule*: This determines what is and what is not a possible syntactic rule.
- Definition of a *possible grammar* (grammar as a set of rules): Not just any set of rules counts as a possible grammar.

Is this an adequate theory of language acquisition, even if the two definitions are made precise? Well, no. It's the beginning of a theory of language acquisition, but in the *Aspects* model there are just too many possible rules and grammars available to the child. In order to address this problem, Chomsky proposed the following concept:

- An *evaluation metric*

The evaluation metric is a procedure that looks at all the possible grammars compatible with the data the child has been exposed to and ranks them. On the basis of some criterion, it says that G_1 is a more highly valued grammar than G_2, and it picks G_1, even though G_1 and G_2 are both compatible with the data.

For the moment, think of a language as a set of sentences, and think of a grammar as a formal device for generating all and only those sentences. Now, what is the child's task? Born not knowing what the grammar is, and confronted with some primary linguistic data (PLD), the child makes a guess about what the grammar is. And the guess has to be such that it will generate the PLD. It will invariably generate more than the PLD. Why? Because a human grammar has to provide an infinite language. That is the strongest linguistic universal there is. All human languages are infinite. That guarantees that whatever the child's guess is, it will generate vastly more than the (necessarily finite) PLD.

Suppose a child's guess is a grammar G_1 that generates a language L_1 (PLD a subset of L_1). Now, one can imagine a second child being exposed to exactly the same PLD and coming up with a grammar G_2 that is compatible with the PLD and generates $L_2 \neq L_1$. And let's say a third child comes up with grammar G_3 that generates L_3. Suppose that all these languages, an infinite class of them, agree on the PLD and disagree on virtually everything else. This is the most extreme case (to make the point clear), represented in (114).

(114)

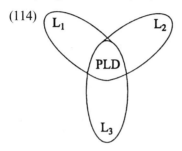

So, these grammars are compatible with the PLD (and, by hypothesis, with the formal constraints on possible grammars); hence, all are available to the child as potential grammars. But suppose that G_3 (generating L_3) is the grammar valued most highly by the evaluation metric. Then, when confronted with the PLD, the child is forced to posit G_3, the grammar valued most highly by the evaluation metric that is also compatible with the PLD. This will give the presumably correct result that learners confronted with the same data will acquire the same language; in other words, the situation depicted above, where three children exposed to the same PLD arrive at different grammars, can't arise.

What exactly is the evaluation metric? This is something we don't know a priori (a point that is often seriously misunderstood). It's an *empirical* question. It's the same kind of question as asking what's a possible rule, or what's a possible grammar. Chomsky made proposals about possible rules (he formalized the notion of PS rule, of transformational rule) and a possible grammar (some specific arrangement of these PS rules and transformations). He further proposed that the evaluation metric is this: Given two permissible grammars G_1 and G_2 both compatible with the PLD, G_1 is more highly valued than G_2 if and only if G_1 has fewer symbols than G_2.

With this in mind, let's return to the arrangements of auxiliary verbs. Chomsky proposed in *Syntactic Structures* that there is always at least one item in Aux position, and that that item is there whether or not the structure has any auxiliary verbs. The first item in Aux is always the symbol C (= tense and agreement information; later we'll look at C in much more detail). If so, then instead of the PS rules in (113) we have the ones in (115).

(115) Aux → C
      Aux → C M
      Aux → C HAVE
      Aux → C BE
      Aux → C M HAVE
      Aux → C M BE
      Aux → C HAVE BE
      Aux → C M HAVE BE

Chomsky made the following empirical claim: It's very natural for a language to have the eight rules we've been discussing, rather than some random eight rules for Aux. After all, we could imagine all kinds of different sets of eight rules using these symbols. So, we want to introduce some notation that will allow the evaluation metric to give us the result that the rules in (115) form a natural set. The notation also will be wired in, of course.

Here's the notation that Chomsky proposed:

(116) Aux → C (M) (HAVE) (BE)

What does this notation mean? It represents exactly the eight rules we've been discussing, but counted by the evaluation metric as having the cost of only one rule: Aux → C M HAVE BE. Informally speaking, M, HAVE, and BE in (116) are each optional.

This move seems seductively natural, but one could imagine that the world could have been otherwise. Imagine a language that has the following rules for auxiliaries:

(117) Aux → C M HAVE BE
      Aux → C HAVE BE M
      Aux → C BE M HAVE

As far as I know, no language on earth is like that. But maybe Martian is. One may think, then, that Martian is impossible to characterize, because the notation we used for English doesn't work there. But in fact, it could be characterized. We just have to make up a new notation. One natural possibility is this:

(118)

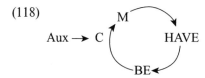

By using this notation, we're saying that the three rules in (117) count as no more expensive than any one of them. Why is this a natural notation? Because what comes after C is a set of *cyclic permutations* of M, BE, and HAVE: first pick any one of the elements on the circle, and continue clockwise until all of them are taken.

Mathematically, there's nothing to choose between (116) and (118). A mathematician might want to use the notation in (118); and the study of cyclic permutations is an area of mathematics. It's only *for empirical reasons* that we choose the notation in (116). In other words, the fact that we choose (116) means that Chomsky's notation has nothing to do with mathematical "elegance" or formal possibility; instead, it has to do with empirical facts of human languages.

(116) is the core of the analysis of auxiliaries presented in *Syntactic Structures*. It wasn't until *Aspects* that Chomsky explicitly claimed that the notation is wired in, but the claim was implicit in the earlier work.

The rule in (116) embodies a generalization about the gross order of M, HAVE, and BE. But there are a lot of finer generalizations about how M, HAVE, and BE are actually realized. Recall that M, HAVE, and BE take on a lot of different forms. Even if we know that M, HAVE, and BE occur in the order specified in (116), what tells us which *instances* of M, HAVE, BE—and, finally, V—can actually occur? Here, Chomsky argued that we need something more powerful than just PS rules to account for all of the facts.

1.3.2 Verbal Morphology: More Generalizations

A further look at the examples with which section 1.3.1 began will lead us to the next step. In particular, we will now look more carefully at the finer details of the verbal morphology of English. First let's consider the following alternations:

(119) John sings/sang
       John is/was singing
       John has/had sung
       John can/could sing

Here we seem to have four present/past alternations, holding the subject constant. It's a little tricky to prove that *can/could* is a present/past alternation as opposed to two separate modals. But Chomsky suggested an argument that this is the case, based on a phenomenon often called *sequence of tenses*.

(120) a. John says he owns a house
      b. John said he owned a house

(120b) is ambiguous. One reading is that John said, "I own a house"; the other is that John said, "I owned a house." Similarly for the following examples:

(121) a. John said he is tired
      b. John said he was tired
(122) a. John says he has solved the problem
      b. John said he had solved the problem

When the main verb is past tense, past tense on the embedded verb can be understood as present with respect to the time of the main clause, alongside the expected past tense interpretation. Now note that (123b), with a modal, shows just the same ambiguity.

(123) a. John says he can/will swim
      b. John said he could/would swim

So there's some reason for thinking that Chomsky's treatment of modals as showing tense alternations is correct. Thus, we'll assume here that modals do take tense. Ultimately nothing crucial will depend on this treatment, but it's the one that Chomsky gave, so for consistency, and in the absence of a strong counterargument, we'll adopt it too.

Now consider sentences with no auxiliary verbs.

(124) a. John owns a house   present
      b. John owned a house   past
      c. *John own a house   bare
      d. *John owning a house   progressive
      e. *John owned a house   perfect

Here's the generalization that describes these cases:

(125) *Generalization I*

      If the main verb is the first "verblike thing" in the sentence, then it can appear in the "present" or "past" form, but not in the "bare" or "progressive" or "perfect" form.

We have to tease apart "past" and "perfect," which are often phonologically identical. By putting a star on (124e) as opposed to (124b), we're assuming that the "past" and the "perfect" are different. (126) will make this clearer.

(126) a. John writes   present
      b. John wrote   past
      c. *John write   bare
      d. *John writing   progressive
      e. *John written   perfect

The perfect form of *write* in (126e) is different from the past form of *write* in (126b). This is the beginning of an argument to show that the past is generally different from the perfect even though in (124) they have the same phonological form.

■ *Gutiérrez:* Suppose we have a sentence like *I write.* Do we say that this is the bare form? Or do we say that it's the present form, but that the present form and the bare form are phonologically equivalent?

Lasnik: Yes, that's a very important question. Chomsky gave a compelling answer to that question in *Syntactic Structures* showing that there's indeed a "zero morpheme" in a case like that.[9]   ■

Can we extend Generalization I to other types of sentences? What's special about a sentence with no auxiliaries is that the main verb is the first "verblike thing." What we want to do is to investigate whether something like Generalization I holds for other things that might happen to be the first "verblike thing" in a sentence. By "verblike thing" we mean, in addition to a verb, a modal or HAVE or BE. For Chomsky, crucially, modals, HAVE, and BE aren't verbs at all—that's why I'm calling them "verblike things."

So let's consider sentences with one auxiliary, starting with HAVE. What forms of HAVE can occur when it's the first "verblike thing" in the sentence?

(127) a. John has written   present
      b. John had written   past
      c. *John have written   bare
      d. *John having written   progressive
      e. *John had written   perfect[10]

The generalization that covers these cases is similar to Generalization I.

(128) *Generalization I'*

> If HAVE is the first "verblike thing" in the sentence, then it can appear in the "present" or "past" form, but not in the "bare" or "progressive" or "perfect" form.

What happens when the first "verblike thing" in a sentence is BE?

(129) a.   John is writing   present
      b.   John was writing   past
      c.   *John be writing   bare
      d.   *John being writing   progressive
      e.   *John been writing   perfect

The generalization that describes these cases is very similar to Generalizations I and I'.

(130) *Generalization I''*

> If BE is the first "verblike thing" in the sentence, then it can appear in the "present" or "past" form, but not in the "bare" or "progressive" or "perfect" form.

Rather trivially, a parallel generalization holds for modals.

(131) a. John can write   present
      b. John could write   past

(132) *Generalization I'''*

> If a modal is the first "verblike thing" in the sentence, then it can appear in the "present" or "past" form and no other form.

Modals seem to trivially fall under Generalization I since they have only present and past forms, and no others, such as a progressive (*canning*), perfect, or bare form. (Bare forms can occur after *to* in the infinitive construction in English, so we can say *to write* or *to be able to*, but we can't say **to can*.)

Putting all these specific generalizations together, we have the following overall generalization:

(133) *Generalization I+*

> Whatever "verblike thing" is the first in a sentence, it will appear in the "present" or "past" form.

Can we find any generalization about the *second* "verblike thing" in a sentence? Consider the following examples:

(134) a. He can go   bare
      b. He is singing   progressive
      c. He has written   perfect
      d. *He can goes   present
      e. *He can went   past

The second "verblike thing" can be progressive, perfect, or bare. But it cannot be past or present. Abstractly, English sentences can have these sequences of two "verblike things":

(135) BE V
       M V
       HAVE V

The form of the second "verblike thing" depends on what the preceding "verblike thing" is. One combination is "BE + progressive."

(136) a. John is singing
      b. John was singing

A second is "modal + bare."

(137) a. John can swim
      b. John could swim

A third is "HAVE + perfect."

(138) a. John has written
      b. John had written

From these facts, we can deduce Generalization II.

(139) *Generalization II*
      a. When a sentence has two "verblike things" and the first is
          HAVE, then the second appears in the "perfect" form.
      b. When a sentence has two "verblike things" and the first is BE,
          then the second appears in the "progressive" form.
      c. When a sentence has two "verblike things" and the first is a
          modal, then the second appears in the "bare" form.

What happens when a sentence has three "verblike things" and the first is HAVE? As (140) shows, the "verblike thing" that follows HAVE still appears in the perfect form.

(140) a. John has been writing
      b. John had been writing

Finally, what if a sentence has more than three "verblike things"?

(141) John could have been writing

The generalization is the same. We can therefore state the following overall generalization:

(142) *Generalization II*$^+$
Whenever HAVE occurs, the very next "verblike thing" appears in the "perfect" form.

Now let's look at modals. What kind of thing can come after a modal? (143) gives some examples, and (144) the generalization we can draw from them.

(143) a. John must write
b. John must have left
c. John must be singing

(144) *Generalization III*
Whenever a modal occurs, the very next "verblike thing" appears in the "bare" form.

Finally, let's look at BE. What kind of thing can follow BE? (For the moment I'll abstract away from sentences like *John is tall* and *John was arrested*, which are sentences where BE seems to be the only "verblike thing.")

(145) a. John is sleeping
b. John was sleeping
c. John has been sleeping
d. John may be sleeping
e. John may have been sleeping

The generalization we can draw about BE is the following:

(146) *Generalization IV*
Whenever BE occurs, the very next "verblike thing" appears in the "progressive" form.

So, when a sentence has BE, it has *ing* (progressive). When a sentence has HAVE, it has *en* (perfect). When a sentence has M, it has the bare form. BE and *ing* do *go* together, but they don't go *together*. There's something in between. HAVE and *en* do *go* together, but they don't go *together*. There's something in between. We have a paradox. The rule that

Chomsky proposed to resolve the first part of the paradox, the dependency, is the following, an extension of (116):

(147) Aux → C (M) (have en) (be ing)

As before, this rule is an abbreviation of eight rules. First, as before, C (tense-agreement morphology) precedes the first "verblike thing." Second, this rule correctly guarantees that *have* and *en* are always introduced together, and similarly for *be* and *ing*. But notice that *have* actually introduces the perfect form of the *next* "verblike thing" and *be* introduces the progressive form of the *next* "verblike thing." This situation is shown in (148).

(148)

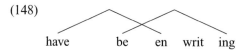

     have   be   en   writ   ing

(148) represents a *cross-serial dependency*. PS rules can't in general deal with these dependencies; they're good at characterizing *nested* dependencies, as we saw, but not cross-serial ones.

To see this point, recall what a derivation is in a PS grammar. It's a sequence of lines, such that the first line is the designated initial symbol, maybe S, we derive the second line from the first by rewriting one occurrence of one symbol, and we keep going until we reach symbols that can't be rewritten. The symbols that can't be rewritten, the terminal symbols, are those that don't occur on the left-hand side of any arrow.

Let's see just how effective a PS grammar is in capturing the generalizations discussed above. Suppose we want to generate the following sentence:

(149) John might have been kissing Mary

We'll be using Chomsky's PS rules (page 111 of *Syntactic Structures*), but we'll add two more rules just to simplify the derivations.

(150) NP$_{sing}$ → John
      NP$_{sing}$ → Mary

The PS rules give us the following derivation, among numerous possible ones:

(151) S
      NP VP
      NP Verb NP

NP Aux V NP
NP_{sing} Aux V NP

NP$_{sing}$ Aux V NP
NP$_{sing}$ C M have en be ing V NP
John C M have en be ing V NP
John C M have en be ing V NP$_{sing}$
John C M have en be ing V Mary
John C may have en be ing V Mary
John C may have en be ing kiss Mary

We already know that if we collapse all the equivalent derivations, we get the PM for the sentence in (149). Let's look at (152), the collapsed PS tree.

(152)

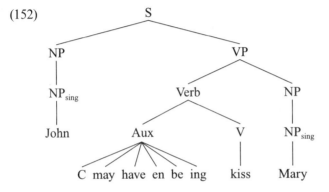

Apparently, we end up with something that we don't want to generate.

(153) John C may have en be ing kiss Mary

(152) captures the fact that *have* and *en* are introduced together, but not that *en* ends up on *be*. It captures the fact that *be* and *ing* are also introduced together, but not that *ing* ends up on *kiss*. The question is, how can we rectify this? With PS rules we can't generate this sentence in any illuminating way. The best we can do with PS rules is to list all the cases. Chomsky argued on this basis that we need a device more powerful than PS rules, a device that's capable of capturing these paradoxical regularities.

Chapter 2

Transformational Grammar

2.1 WHAT IS A TRANSFORMATION?

We need something more powerful than PS rules to account for cross-serial dependencies. This more powerful device will let us rearrange the PS representation, changing one PS representation into another. In (152) of chapter 1 we have the PS representation that we got from applying the PS rules. We want to rearrange this PS representation so that *en* is attached to *be* and *ing* is attached to *kiss*.[1]

This more powerful device that changes one PS representation into another PS representation is called a *transformation*. In this case the relevant transformation takes each of the verbal affixes and attaches it to the following "verblike thing."

Now we need to extend our notion of derivation. What is a derivation? A derivation begins with a sequence of lines given by PS rules (or a set of such sequences). This sequence results in a PM, which we may call the *initial PM*. Then we can apply some transformation that takes as its input an initial PM and gives as its output a sort of PM as well. Just like an initial PM, this *derived PM* must be something that determines the constituent structure of a sentence. We don't want to distinguish sharply between the notions of initial and derived PM because what's special about transformational grammar as formalized here is that transformations *don't* care whether the structures at issue are PMs or derived PMs. When the distinction isn't relevant, I will thus revert to conventional usage and use the term *PM* to refer to both the output of the PS derivation and the output of particular transformations.

Recall too from the earlier informal discussion (section 1.1) that movement is assumed to be structure dependent. If there's ever a case where more than one transformation can apply in the derivation of a sentence, the output of the first transformation must be of exactly the same formal character as the input; otherwise, the second transformation won't have the units that it needs in order to apply properly. Our theory needs to require that in a derivation like (1) the successive *derived constituent structures* (PM_2, PM_3, PM_4) be formally of the same character as the initial structure (PM_1), so that the successive transformations (T_2, T_3) can take them as input.

(1) $PM_1 \xrightarrow{T_1} PM_2 \xrightarrow{T_2} PM_3 \xrightarrow{T_3} PM_4$

So far the major argument for transformational derivation has been that there are properties of human languages that can't be explained with PS grammars (they can be *stated*, but they can't be *explained*). Another classic argument for transformations involves "felt-relatedness" between sentences. For example:

(2) a. John is singing
    b. Is John singing?

(3) a. John sings
    b. Does John sing?

(4) a. I like linguistics
    b. Linguistics, I like

If our only evidence were these cases and we were just working at this intuitive level of "felt-relatedness," we could be misled into incorrectly characterizing what transformations are in this system; namely, we could conclude, incorrectly, that they directly relate sentences to other sentences.

Chomsky's transformations do *not* relate sentences to other sentences; they relate one abstract structure (a PM) to another abstract structure (another PM). Often as a by-product of relating abstract structures, we will find an explanation for felt-relatedness between sentences, but transformations don't "transform" sentences into other sentences. Interestingly, there was an earlier influential formulation of transformational grammar—due to Zellig Harris, Chomsky's teacher—that did explicitly relate sentences to other sentences.[2] Because it did so, it wasn't able to give any systematic explanation for the kind of phenomena we're dealing with now. To deal with these phenomena requires the ability to relate abstract structures to abstract structures. To put it another way, the phenomena we've begun looking at provide evidence that sentences have abstract underlying structures.

With that in mind, let's begin to see how the theory of transformations is formalized. It wasn't fully formalized in *Syntactic Structures* (which was really just Chomsky's lecture notes), but it was fully formalized in *LSLT*.

2.2   A FIRST LOOK AT TRANSFORMATIONS: THE NUMBER AND AUXILIARY TRANSFORMATIONS T15 AND T20

Let's begin to look at some transformations responsible for the rearrangements we've been discussing. In particular, consider the Number Transformation T15 and the Auxiliary Transformation T20 (standardly called *Affix Hopping*) from page 112 of *Syntactic Structures.* (SA = structural analysis; SC = structural change)

T15 Number Transformation (obligatory)
SA: X – C – Y
SC: C $\rightarrow$ s in the context NP_{sing} _____
$\quad\quad\quad$ $\varnothing$ in other contexts
$\quad\quad\quad$ *past* in any context

T20 Auxiliary Transformation (obligatory)
SA: X – "Af" – "v" – Y (where "*Af*" is any C or is *en* or *ing*; "*v*" is
$\quad\quad$ any M or V, or *have* or *be*)
SC: $X_1 - X_2 - X_3 - X_4 \rightarrow X_1 - X_3 - X_2 \# - X_4$

(The notation # means that a word boundary is added.)

This is what Chomsky's PS grammar on page 111 tells us about the sentence *John left*:

(5)

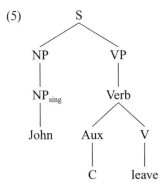

(To allow for intransitives I've added the rule VP $\rightarrow$ Verb to Chomsky's VP $\rightarrow$ Verb NP.)

The Number Transformation tells us what the tense is going to be. It's the only transformation in *Syntactic Structures* that looks like a PS rule. This raises the question of why Chomsky didn't analyze this operation as part of the PS grammar. It's because of a limitation that Chomsky imposed on the PS component of the grammar: he wanted all the PS rules to be *context free*. The Number Transformation is a PS rule, but it is crucially *context sensitive*.

Applying the Number Transformation to (5), we get (6).

(6)

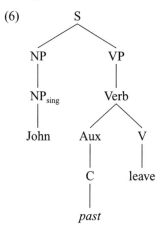

As for Affix Hopping, it will attach *past* to *leave* in (6). The graphic representation of the new PM will be (7), thanks to an operation Chomsky called *adjunction*. When *past* adjoins to V, the adjunction process creates a new instance of V that dominates both the original V and *past*.[3]

(7)

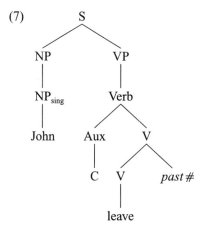

Let's now look at the transformational portion of the derivation of the sentence in (8).

(8) John will be sleeping

We start with the initial PM in (9).

(9)

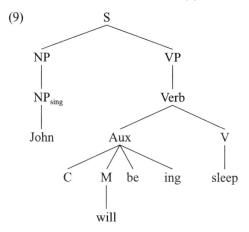

Applying the Number Transformation to the PM in (9), we obtain (10).

(10)

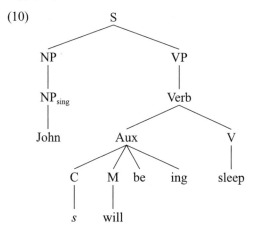

Now, applying Affix Hopping to the PM in (10), we finally obtain (11).[4]

(11)

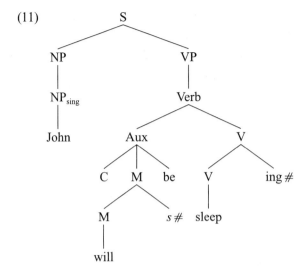

2.3   PROPERTIES OF TRANSFORMATIONS

Transformations have numerous formal properties. First, each transformation has a *structural analysis* (SA) and a *structural change* (SC). The SA characterizes the class of structures to which the transformation applies. It tells us the class of "PM-like things" that are able to undergo the process. The SC specifies the alterations that the process carries out. It tells us what happens to a particular element that is eligible to undergo the process when the process applies (e.g., move, delete, add something).

2.3.1   Structural Analysis

2.3.1.1   What Constitutes a Structural Analysis

Let's look at SAs in more detail. An SA is a sequence of *terms*, or a set of sequences of terms, as in the SA of T16 (T_{not}, usually called the *Negation Transformation*), T17 (T_A, or *Affirmation*), and T18 (T_q, or *Subject Aux(iliary) Inversion*), shown here (see *Syntactic Structures*, page 112).[5]

(12) *T16–T18 Negation Transformation, Affirmation, Subject-Aux Inversion*
SA: a. NP – C – V X
     b. NP – C + M – X
     c. NP – C + have – X
     d. NP – C + be – X

Term refers to material set off by hyphens in Chomsky's notation. Elements that can potentially constitute a term are listed in (13).

(13) a. A single nonterminal symbol, like Aux, NP, V, or NP
   b. A single terminal symbol, like C before the Number Transformation T15 applies (after it applies, C is *no longer* a terminal symbol)
   c. A variable, like X or Y
   d. A sequence of nonterminal symbols, like C + M in (12b)
   e. A sequence of terminal and nonterminal symbols, like C + *have* in (12c)
   f. A sequence of nonterminal and variable symbols, as in (12a)

We can summarize these cases as follows:

(14) a. Any sequence of symbols (terminals, nonterminals, and variables) *or*
   b. A set of sequences of symbols *or*
   c. A Boolean combination of these

Now consider the terms in Affix Hopping T20. The SA is as follows:

(15) X – "Af" – "v" – Y

There are apparently four terms in this SA. X and Y are variables. But what are "Af" and "v"? "Af" and "v" aren't terms of the grammar. They aren't terminal or nonterminal symbols; nor are they variables. "Af" is trying to suggest that C and *en*, or *ing*, are of the same category, even though the grammar doesn't say this. Similarly, "v" suggests that M, V, *have*, and *be* are of the same category, though again, the grammar doesn't give this result (more on this later).

2.3.1.2 Formalization of the Structural Analysis

The SA of a transformation specifies what kind of PM can undergo the transformation. To begin to formalize the notion of SA, let's see how the SA formally carries out the task of determining, for a given PM, whether the transformation is eligible to apply or not. Let's look at the SA for the Passive Transformation T12.

(16) NP – Aux – V – NP

To see whether the Passive Transformation applies to a PM, we first have to have a PM. So, let's construct one. For pedagogical purposes, first we'll construct it in the form of a tree, shown in (17), and then we'll construct it as a set because Chomsky's formalization of transformations was based not on trees, but on sets.

(17)

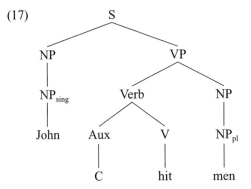

(Assume, for simplification, the following extra rules: $NP_{sing} \rightarrow$ *John*, $NP_{pl} \rightarrow$ *men*.)

(17) is the initial PM, the output of the PS rules. What sentence is this the initial PM for? There are scores of them. Here are some (just impressionistically—in a moment we'll see how the formalism supports this):

(18) a. John hits men
     b. John hit men

(19) a. Men are hit by John
     b. Men were hit by John

(20) a. Does John hit men?
     b. Did John hit men?
     c. Are men hit by John?
     d. Were men hit by John?

(21) a. John doesn't hit men
     b. John didn't hit men
     c. Men weren't hit by John
     d. Men aren't hit by John
        etc.

Now let's construct the set-theoretic object that is the true PM in this theory.

(22) PM = {S, NP VP, NP_{sing} VP, John VP, John C hit men, NP V NP, NP_{sing} Aux hit NP_{pl}, John C V men, NP_{sing} Aux V NP_{pl}, NP Aux V NP, ...}

Now we're in a position to determine whether the particular transformation is applicable to the structure. Here's what we do. With the SA for the transformation in hand, we search through the PM (initial or derived). If we find an element in the PM that *satisfies* the SA, then we can apply the transformation (and we *must* if the rule is marked obligatory, a point I'll return to immediately). What does satisfaction mean? Satisfaction is *identity*, with one exception, namely, a variable. Indeed, anything can satisfy X. For the Passive Transformation to apply, we must find an element of the PM that is exactly $NP - Aux - V - NP$. If we find it, we can apply the rule; if we don't, then we can't. That is satisfaction in this case. In the PM (22) we do find that element, so we can apply the rule (but need not, since this transformation is optional). I put aside the effects of this transformation.

Now look at the Number Transformation T15, whose SA is (23).

(23) $X - C - Y$

X and Y are variables. Anything at all can satisfy X or Y. C, on the other hand, is a constant term.

Let's find an element of the PM in (22) that satisfies the SA of the Number Transformation. One such element is this:

(24) John C V men

John satisfies X, *C* satisfies C, *V men* satisfies Y.

If a rule's SA is satisfied, and the rule is optional, we can either apply or not apply the rule. What happens when the rule is obligatory, as the Number Transformation is? There are two imaginable senses of *obligatory*. One is the sense in which we *must* apply a certain rule and it doesn't matter whether the PM is the right kind or not; if this rule isn't applied, the derivation won't be good. This isn't Chomsky's sense, however. His sense is that if a rule's SA is satisfied, then we have to apply the rule, but if it isn't, then we don't. It is thus the weaker of the two senses of *obligatory*; we only *have to* apply the rule if we're *able* to. Even in this weaker sense, we will always have to apply the Number Transformation, because C will be introduced into every derivation.

2.3.2 Structural Change

Having looked at SA in more detail, let's look now at SC, again using the Number Transformation T15 and the Auxiliary Transformation (Affix Hopping) T20 as illustration.

2.3.2.1 The Number and Auxiliary Transformations Again

Consider the initial PM for the sentence *John left*. Its graphic representation is shown in (25).

(25)

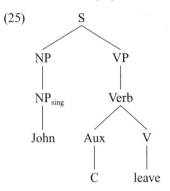

The first thing we want to determine is whether the Number Transformation T15 is eligible to apply. (25) is a graphic representation of set (26).

(26) {S, NP VP, NP$_{sing}$ VP, John VP, NP Verb, NP$_{sing}$ Verb, John Verb, NP Aux V, NP Aux leave, NP C V, NP C leave, NP$_{sing}$ Aux V, NP$_{sing}$ Aux leave, NP$_{sing}$ C V, NP$_{sing}$ C leave, John Aux V, John Aux leave, John C V, John C leave}

Set (26) contains many elements satisfying the SA of the Number Transformation (see (23)): "anything" followed by C followed by "anything." For example, we find in the set the element *NP C leave*. (This is one of the lines in at least one of the PS derivations.) From this, we can see that the SA is satisfied because NP satisfies X (anything satisfies X), *C* satisfies C (*C* is the only thing that satisfies C, because C is a constant term), and *leave* satisfies Y (anything satisfies Y).

Now recall what the SC for the Number Transformation looks like.

(27) *T15 Number Transformation*
  SC: C → *s* in the context NP$_{sing}$[6]
    $\emptyset$ in other contexts
    past in any context

The SC of the Number Transformation as stated in (27) gives us a choice. Let's take the third option: *past*. What the SC does to the PM in (25) is graphically represented in (28).

(28)

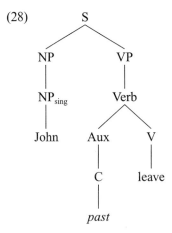

Now the question is, what does the Number Transformation do to the *set*? Everything that was in the set before is still there; but some new elements will be added. Here are two of them:

(29) a. NP$_{sing}$ *past* leave
    b. John *past* leave

In fact, there will be six new elements in the new (derived) PM. They will all have the form "something – *past* – something"; the first "something" will be either NP, NP$_{sing}$, or *John*, and the second "something" will be either *leave* or V. The old PM is thus a proper subset of the new PM. This is a very rare case; it only happens when the transformation is more like a PS rule. In all other cases the PM is radically altered.

Let's look at a more complicated case. Suppose we've applied the Number Transformation, deriving (28) as our new PM, and now we want to apply Affix Hopping (Auxiliary Transformation) T20. First let's see graphically what Affix Hopping is supposed to do; then we'll speculate about what changes take place in the set. We'll see that even for such a simple transformation, there's a dramatic change in the set.

Recall the SC for Affix Hopping.

(30) *T20 Affix Hopping*
    SC: $X_1 - X_2 - X_3 - X_4 \rightarrow X_1 - X_3 - X_2 \# - X_4$

Chomsky's intention was that after applying Affix Hopping, we'll end up with the tree in (31).

(31)

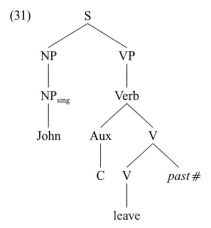

The transformation takes *past* away from C and adjoins it to V, in such a way that *leave* and *past* together constitute a V. (Additionally, recall that a word boundary # is added.)

■ *Chen:*   Why do we end up with two Vs? Is there any empirical evidence for doing things this way?

Lasnik: Chomsky wanted to say that just as the stem was a V before we did the operation, the stem is still a V after we did the operation. There's no reason to sacrifice this information. But we certainly also want to capture the fact (the semantics and morphophonemics demand this) that *leave + past* is also a V.[7]   ■

What Chomsky calls "adjunction" is the attachment of α to β in such a way that α and β together constitute a β. (32) shows *right* adjunction of α to β.[8]

(32)

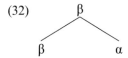

This is consistent with something we'll see again and again in Chomsky's formulation of transformational grammar: namely, that transformations don't gratuitously take away information. The information that *leave* is a V was in the structure, and unless the transformation explicitly says to take away that information, it won't. Transformations preserve structural information, to the extent possible. In the case of the Number Transformation, *all* structural information was preserved. In the case of Affix

Hopping as applied in (31), some structural information is lost: the information that *past* is a C. We don't lose the information that *leave* is a V; nor, of course, do we have to lose the information that *John* is an NP or that *John* is an NP$_{sing}$, so all of that is preserved.

Chomsky had critics in the '60s who said, "These transformations aren't explicit enough. They don't say exactly what the new structure should look like—they only tell a few tiny details about it." That's not a valid criticism. In fact, it's really praise. What Chomsky had in mind was that the vast majority of the properties of the new structure are predicted on general grounds. We don't want a dictionary, in the entry of every word, to say that it's a word. Since that's a general property of all the entries, we don't waste space in the dictionary mentioning it over and over again. In the same way, we don't want a particular transformation to say something that's predicted on general grounds; we don't waste "space" in the grammar specifying things in particular transformations that are general to *all* transformations. Let me give three examples. First, if a portion of the structure isn't involved in the transformation, nothing in that substructure is changed. Second, if for example NP is targeted by a movement rule, the position of the NP changes, but its internal structure is unaffected. Third, if the relevant terms of the transformation are all internal to one constituent, they'll still all be internal to that constituent in the output.

How does pre–Affix Hopping (28) compare to post–Affix Hopping (31) set-theoretically? (33) lists three elements in the set graphically represented by (31) that were also in the set graphically represented by (28).

(33) NP VP
      NP$_{sing}$ VP
      S

What are some new elements in the set?

(34) NP Aux V *past*
      John C leave *past*

(Notice that C keeps switching back and forth. It was a terminal symbol in (25), then it wasn't a terminal symbol in (28), and then it was a terminal symbol again in (31). This fact is a curiosity, but as far as I can tell, of no particular importance.)

What are some elements that were part of the PM in (28) but are no longer part of the PM in (31)?

(35) NP *past* leave

 John Aux leave

We've seen that in general there are dramatic differences between the set-theoretic representations of the structure before and after applying a transformation. The algorithm specifying what the new PM will look like gets rather complicated. Chomsky formalized it one way; Lasnik and Kupin (1977) formalized it a slightly different way. The details won't concern us here.

2.3.2.2 Formalization of Structural Change

Let's look at the kinds of operations that Chomsky took the SCs to be capable of carrying out. These are the *elementary operations* listed in (36).

(36) a. Adjunction of one term to another (to the right or to the left)

 b. Deletion of a term or sequence of terms (e.g., *Mary will solve the problem and Ann will too*, where it seems we've deleted *solve the problem*)

 c. Adjunction of new material (that wasn't in the structure before) to a term (This forms the crux of Chomsky's analysis of *Did John leave?*; the *do* part of *did* is adjoined to something in the structure. The Negation Transformation T16 also has this effect; it adjoins *n't* into the structure.)

 d. Permutation (changing the order of two items without attaching either one to the other). In the simplest case, we can think of the tree as a mobile; we can spin part of it and change the order of certain elements.

An SC for Chomsky was a (possibly ordered) set of elementary operations (Chomsky sometimes called them *elementary transformations*). For example, Affix Hopping T20 carries out one elementary operation, adjunction. Subject-Auxiliary Inversion T18 carries out one elementary operation, permutation. The Negation Transformation carries out the elementary operation of adjoining new material to a term. The Passive Transformation T12 carries out a number of elementary operations.

2.4 OTHER PROPERTIES OF TRANSFORMATIONS

2.4.1 Numbers and Order

What other properties are central to transformations? Notice the numbers that each of them are assigned. Those might seem as unimportant as the names, but they aren't. The fact that the Passive Transformation is T12 and the Number Transformation is T15 is important. If we want to apply both transformations, we must apply T12 before T15. The rules are *ordered*, and this is significant.

Chomsky's Passive Transformation has the effect of ultimately relating *John hit the men* and *The men were hit by John*. Now, this statement can be misleading since, as I mentioned before, Chomsky's transformations don't actually turn sentences into other sentences. They turn PMs into other PMs, and sometimes it turns out that two sentences arise from the same initial PM. Suppose (37a) and (37b) are ultimately related by a transformation, namely, the Passive Transformation.

(37) a. John owns the houses
     b. The houses are owned by John

Now note that the number agreement on the verb in (37b) is determined by *the houses*. But suppose that we applied T15, the Number Transformation, before T12, the Passive Transformation. Instead of (37b), we would get (38).

(38) *The houses is owned by John

In (38) agreement was incorrectly determined by the singular NP *John*, which was formerly in subject position. The important point, then, is that ordering is significant.

2.4.2 Obligatoriness

Transformations are specified as being optional or obligatory. For some transformations it's crucial that we be *allowed* to apply them but not *required* to apply them; for others it's crucial that we be required to apply them. The latter is true particularly of the transformation that will solve our cross-serial dependency problem. If that one weren't obligatory, then it wouldn't be obligatory to separate *have* and *en*. However, we know by just looking at the facts of English, such as those in (40), that even though we've introduced *have* and *en* together (see (39)), they always wind up separated—so the process that separates them has to be obligatory.

(39) John C must have en leave

(40) a. *John must had leave
     b. John must have left

Intuitively, we know that *have* and *en* must go together, but also that they must not go together. The intuition is that superficially *have* and *en* never go together, but "deep down" they always go together.

The idea of a "deep down" representation was brand new in Chomsky's transformational grammar. For Harris, too, sentences had structure, but each sentence just had one structure. What we're heading toward is the idea that a sentence has more than one structure: a more abstract structure that captures some aspects of it, a more superficial structure that captures others, and many structures in between, assuming that many transformations can apply.

2.4.3   Global Dependency

T19 (called T_w in *Syntactic Structures*—the rule creating and fronting interrogative expressions like *who*) is optional and conditional on T18 (T_q, commonly called *Subject-Auxiliary Inversion*—the rule permuting the subject and a portion of Aux). To apply T19, we have to look back and see if T18 has applied. I don't want to try to formalize this kind of global dependency since it will be one of the first things we will throw out of the system, because it gives so much excess descriptive power. If any stage of a derivation could refer back to any other stage of a derivation, just imagine what we could describe.

2.5   TRANSFORMATIONS IN *SYNTACTIC STRUCTURES*

2.5.1   Affix Hopping

2.5.1.1   The Nature of "Af" and "v"

Transformation T20, Affix Hopping, plays a central role in Chomsky's analysis, namely, resolving the paradox of the cross-serial dependencies in English verbal morphology. If (31) correctly illustrates the effect of Affix Hopping, then one instance of Affix Hopping needs to right-adjoin *past* to V, as shown in (41).

(41) SA: X – *past* – V – Y   John *past* leave
           X_1 X_2 X_3 X_4
     SC: $X_1 – X_3 – X_2 \# – X_4$ John left

We can't exactly tell just from looking at the statement of Affix Hopping in *Syntactic Structures* that it's carrying out adjunction rather than permutation, but the discussion in *LSLT* makes it clear. Term 2 right-adjoins to term 3. In addition, this transformation puts a word boundary (#) after term 2. (We'll return to that.)

Let's look at other instances.

(42) SA: X $-$ s $-$ V $-$ Y   John s eat apples
          X$_1$ X$_2$ X$_3$ X$_4$
     SC: X$_1$ $-$ X$_3$ $-$ X$_2$ # $-$ X$_4$ John eats apples

(43) SA: X $-$ past $-$ M $-$ Y   John past can eat
          X$_1$ X$_2$ X$_3$ X$_4$
     SC: X$_1$ $-$ X$_3$ $-$ X$_2$ # $-$ X$_4$ John could eat

(44) SA: X $-$ $\varnothing$ $-$ V $-$ Y   You $\varnothing$ eat apples
          X$_1$ X$_2$ X$_3$ X$_4$
     SC: X$_1$ $-$ X$_3$ $-$ X$_2$ # $-$ X$_4$ You eat apples[9]

(45) SA: X $-$ s $-$ have $-$ Y   John s have en eat apples
          X$_1$ X$_2$ X$_3$ X$_4$
     SC: X$_1$ $-$ X$_3$ $-$ X$_2$ # $-$ X$_4$ John has en eat apples

(46) SA: X $-$ en $-$ V $-$ Y   John has en eat apples
          X$_1$ X$_2$ X$_3$ X$_4$
     SC: X$_1$ $-$ X$_3$ $-$ X$_2$ # $-$ X$_4$ John has eaten apples

Now, notice that in (45) we end up with the structure in (47).

(47)
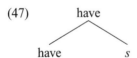

On the other hand, in (46) we end up with the structure in (48),

(48)
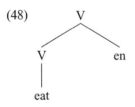

but not the one in (49).

(49)
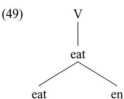

The structure in (49) seems rather outlandish for this case, but it's the same structure we have in (47) for cases like (45). The difference comes from Chomsky's treatment of "auxiliary verbs" as belonging to no syntactic category at all (more on this later).

Let's now collect all of the cases in schematic form, shown in (50).

$$(50) \quad X - \begin{Bmatrix} s \\ past \\ \varnothing \\ en \\ ing \end{Bmatrix} - \begin{Bmatrix} V \\ M \\ have \\ be \end{Bmatrix} - Y$$

Remember our definition of *term*. In particular, a term may consist of a Boolean combination of symbols. The second term in (50) is indeed a Boolean combination of symbols.

(51) *s* **or** *past* **or** $\varnothing$ **or** en **or** ing

The third term in (50) is also a Boolean combination.

(52) V **or** M **or** have **or** be

Notice that for the second and third terms in (50) we used the standard notation for Boolean *or*: { }. This bit of notation, like the parentheses, represents an abbreviatory convention. As such, it constitutes an empirical claim about the evaluation metric.

Now recall that the SA of Affix Hopping is stated like this:

(53) X – "Af" – "v" – Y

By "Af" Chomsky meant all the elements in the second term of the SA in (50); and by "v" Chomsky meant all the elements in the third term of the SA in (50), even though the formal theory doesn't actually support this interpretation.

(54) "Af":   *s, past,* $\varnothing$, en, ing
      "v":   V, M, have, be

Why did Chomsky write things this illicit way? There were two reasons. The first isn't very deep: the form he used takes less space on the page. The second reason is that there *must* be a generalization here. Surely, all the elements referred to as "Af" act as term 2 in the SA because they have something in common. Similarly, all of the elements referred to as "v" act as term 3 because they have something in common.

What do we mean when we say that several elements have something in common? Well, we ought to mean that they're of the same category, that they bear the same "is a" relation to something. But here this just isn't true. *en* is just an *en*; *ing* is just an *ing*; *s* is a C, but *en* isn't a C. They don't have anything in common in the formal presentation of the theory.

What about the elements that Chomsky refers to as "v": V, M, *have, be*? *Have* is just *have*; *be* is just *be*; and so on. There ought to be a generalization here. But the grammar in *Syntactic Structures* doesn't capture it. The way the SA of Affix Hopping is stated makes readers think that maybe the grammar does capture it. The problem is that "Af" and "v" aren't symbols of the grammar. That's conceded in the complicated parenthetical phrase following the SA, which is reproduced here with a small correction.

(55) ... where "Af" is any C, or *en* or *ing*, and where "v" is M or V or *have* or *be*

The SA of Affix Hopping is an abbreviation of 20 transformations. There are five possibilities for term 2 and four possibilities for term 3. Mathematically, not empirically, speaking, the choices are totally independent, so there are $5 \times 4 = 20$ possibilities.

The evaluation metric plays a role here. It's true that the SA of Affix Hopping seems costly and seems to miss some generalizations. However, the evaluation metric says it's better to have these 20 rules than 20 rules that have nothing in common structurally. Why is that? Because the X is common to all 20 transformations, so we don't have to count that 20 times; the same is true for Y. The cost of these 20 rules is 11 symbols, instead of the 80 symbols (4×20) we would have if there were 20 transformations. The evaluation metric tells us that it isn't so totally strange to find 20 rules like this.

This still raises the question that was raised most forcefully by Ross (1969a).[10] Why is it that—at least as far as the morphophonemics is concerned—the five things in the second term of (50) behave so similarly? Why do they feel like a natural class? According to this theory they aren't a natural class. The evaluation metric, and the notational device, lets us write any five things we want as the second term in (50). No matter what we put there, the rule is equally highly valued by the evaluation metric. Similarly for the third term in (50). For instance, why are the four things in the third term of the SA in (50) not the following?

(56) $\begin{Bmatrix} V \\ the \\ banana \\ from \end{Bmatrix}$

We'll be astounded if we find a language that has a rule just like Affix Hopping but where term 3 is as I've shown it in (56). But the evaluation metric says that this is exactly as good as term 3 in the SA of Affix Hopping. So, the evaluation metric is leading us in the right direction but isn't forcing us to go far enough. This constitutes an objection to this approach. Chomsky's use of "Af" and "v" disguised the difficulty.

■ *Gutiérrez:*   In order to solve this problem, can't we add the following two PS rules to the grammar?

(57) "Af" → $\begin{Bmatrix} s \\ past \\ \varnothing \\ en \\ ing \end{Bmatrix}$ "v" → $\begin{Bmatrix} V \\ M \\ have \\ be \end{Bmatrix}$

Lasnik: Good question. Let's try to solve the problem with tools already at our disposal. If we add those rules, we *will* introduce "Af" and "v" as symbols of the grammar. Let's see what other changes we'll have to make in our PS rules.

(58) Aux → C ("v") ("v" "Af") ("v" "Af")
     C → "Af"

What's wrong with that? Why didn't Chomsky take this approach? The difficulty is that (58) doesn't state the selectional properties of the auxiliaries and verbs. So, for example, *have* could introduce *en* as in Rule 10 in *Syntactic Structures*, but it could also introduce *s*, *past*, $\varnothing$, and *ing*; *be* could introduce *ing*, but it could also introduce *s*, *past*, $\varnothing$, and *en*. Shortly, we'll look at a technical device introduced in *Aspects* specifically to deal with selectional phenomena like this.   ■

2.5.1.2   Morphology of Affix Hopping
Recall that Affix Hopping T20 creates structures of the following types:

(59) past *hopping onto V*

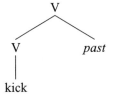

(60) s *hopping onto V*

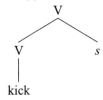

(61) ∅ *hopping onto V*

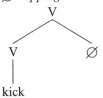

(62) s *hopping onto M*[11]

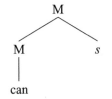

(63) past *hopping onto M*

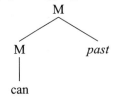

(64) past *hopping onto* have

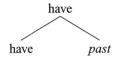

The structure in (64) represents the form *had* (as in *John had left*). Adjunction of *past* to *have* creates a new *have*. This isn't an intuitively obvious result, but it follows from the notion of adjunction combined with the fact that perfective *have* belongs to no category in this system. Similarly, if an *s* adjoins to *have*, the result is *has*, and if a zero morpheme ∅ adjoins to *have*, the result is *have*.

(65) s *hopping onto* have

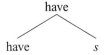

(66) ∅ *hopping onto* have

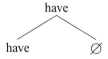

Notice that this system doesn't make enough morphological distinctions when it comes to *be*. Other English verbs have only three different finite forms: one for past, one for third person singular present, and one for all other circumstances, roughly as suggested by Chomsky's Number Transformation T15. But *be* has more forms than that.

(67) Present: am/are/is
     Past: was/were

Thus, the Number Transformation will not be able to generate the paradigm for *be*. It needs to be somewhat richer. I'm not claiming that the syntax tells us exactly how these things are going to be pronounced. But if the syntax produces two objects that are identical, then, in this system, the morphophonemics isn't going to be able to tease them apart.

Another apparent morphological problem is that Affix Hopping looks like it can create forms that don't exist: for example, a modal with *ing* (*maying). Is this a problem or not? Should we try to rewrite this rule or not? Rewriting would be costly; but if we needed to change the rule for descriptive adequacy, we'd be willing to do so. Is this cost necessary? Do we have to rewrite the transformation in a more explicit way to stop the generation of forms like *maying? No, because the PS rules will never produce the sequence that would be transformed into this. The PS rules will never provide an *ing* followed by a modal. It would be redundant to rewrite Affix Hopping so as to exclude that possibility. Since it wouldn't accomplish anything descriptively, and since it would have a significant cost in terms of the evaluation metric, we just don't do it.

2.5.2   Subject-Auxiliary Inversion (T18)

Now consider statement-and-question pairs like these:

(68) a. John was sleeping
     b. Was John sleeping?

(69) a. John can sleep
     b. Can John sleep?

(70) a. John slept
     b. Did John sleep?

Let's start with (68). (71) is the (graphic representation of the) initial PM of *John was sleeping*. It's also the initial PM of *Was John sleeping?*, *Is John sleeping?*, *John is sleeping*, *John isn't sleeping*, and so on. Recall that all these differences are introduced by the transformations, applying to the initial PM that results from doing the PS derivations.

(71)

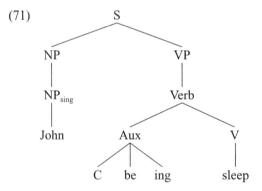

Since we are trying to generate *John was sleeping* and *Was John sleeping?*, we will pick out and apply the right instance of the Number Transformation T15 (C → *past*), and the result will be the PM in (72).

(72)

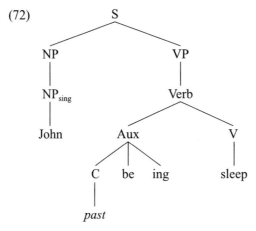

To end up with *John was sleeping*, we apply Affix Hopping T20, which right-adjoins *past* to *be*, and *ing* to *sleep*.[12]

(73)

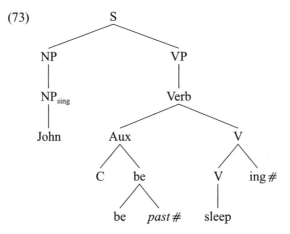

The syntax is now done. The morphophonemics takes over and ensures that *be + past* is pronounced as *was* and that *sleep + ing* is pronounced as *sleeping*.

What if we instead want to end up with *Was John sleeping*? We get this via the Subject-Aux(iliary) Inversion transformation T18. First, though, we'll have to "undo" Affix Hopping, T20, because T18 is ordered before it. There are many reasons for this ordering. Some of them are trivial, some of them are profound, as we will see.

The SA for Subject-Aux Inversion is repeated here (remember that Negation, Affirmation, and Subject-Aux Inversion, T16–T18, all have the same SA):

(74) *T18 Subject-Aux Inversion (optional)*
    SA: a. NP – C – V X
         b. NP – C + M – X
         c. NP – C + have – X
         d. NP – C + be – X

To apply Subject-Aux Inversion to the PM in (72), we want to find out whether any of the four instances of its SA are satisfied there. Is there any element in this PM that satisfies any of the lines (74a–c) of the SA? Apparently, there is none.

There is, however, an element in the PM in (72) that satisfies line (74d) of the SA, namely, *NP C be ing sleep*. NP satisfies NP, C satisfies C, *be* satisfies *be*, and *ing sleep* satisfies X. It doesn't matter that *ing sleep* isn't a constituent or a unit. X is a string variable, not a structure variable. X doesn't have to be a unit of structure; it can just be any string at all. We don't *have* to apply Subject-Aux Inversion, because it's optional, but as long as one element satisfies its SA, then we *can* apply it.

The SC of Subject-Aux Inversion is as follows:

(75) $X_1 - X_2 - X_3 \rightarrow X_2 - X_1 - X_3$

Though we can't tell this just from reading *Syntactic Structures*, Chomsky had in mind a different operation for Subject-Aux Inversion than he did for Affix Hopping. Affix Hopping involves *adjunction*, but Subject-Aux Inversion involves *permutation*. We just change the order of the two first terms, in the simplest possible way (we haven't formalized this permutation set-theoretically).

If the two things we're going to permute are sisters, we can just think of a mobile and the wind, and the process is easy to visualize. However, things are more complicated when the two things we're going to permute aren't sisters, which is definitely the case here with NP and C + *be*. The algorithm (given in *LSLT*) is this: To permute two things that aren't sisters, rearrange them in the specified order in the simplest possible way. In our case, what's the simplest possible way? As far as I can tell, Chomsky took it to be leaving NP in its place and moving C + *be* to the front. This gives the PM in (76).

(76)

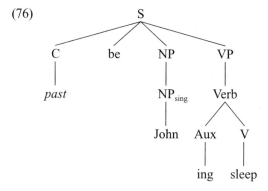

■ *Gutiérrez:*   What prevents us from moving the NP down?

Lasnik: Yes, that's a good question. It's interesting that this didn't become an issue until over 15 years after *Syntactic Structures*, when Chomsky, among others, began to argue that "raising" is to be preferred to "lowering." We'll return to this issue.

Vukić: One argument for Gutiérrez's analysis would be that if we move the NP, we're moving a constituent, but if we move C + *be*, we're not moving a constituent.

Lasnik: Yes, clearly Affix Hopping is affecting a nonconstituent here. C and *be* happen to be next to each other but aren't a unit of structure by themselves. C + *be* is two-thirds of an Aux, and there's no category label on it.

Interestingly, though, in the particular formalism underlying *Syntactic Structures*, the fact that moving NP means moving a constituent and moving C + *be* means moving a nonconstituent isn't relevant. We'd like that distinction to be relevant, and later on we'll start reformalizing some of this material to capture it. It's kind of unpleasant that there can be rules that move nonconstituents. Remember, one of Chomsky's big arguments for structure was that the transformations are structure dependent. What does that mean? To make it formally precise, we'll want to say, "Transformations always affect constituents." If we truly believe in structure dependence, we'd like it to be true that the reason that operations are structure dependent is that the language faculty is wired up in such a way that transformations can only affect constituents. This is a potential explanatory problem of the theory, one that we'll try to overcome later.   ■

Now, we have to try to apply Affix Hopping to (76), since Affix Hopping is obligatory. Since we *can* apply Affix Hopping, we *must* apply it. Applying Affix Hopping will give us the PM in (77).

(77)

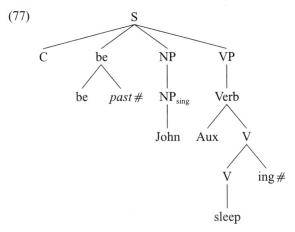

So we've generated *John was sleeping* and *Was John sleeping?* Let's turn now to the pair in (69), *John can sleep* and *Can John sleep?* The initial PM for *John can sleep, Can John sleep?, John can't sleep, Can't John sleep?, John could sleep, Could John sleep?*, and so on, is (78).

(78)

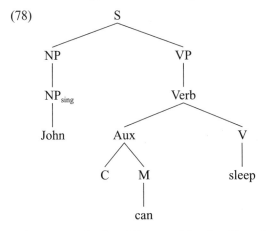

When we apply the obligatory Number Transformation, we get the PM in (79).

(79)

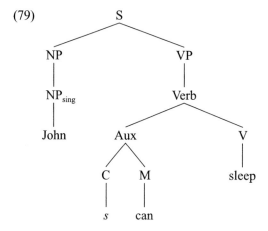

Now let's try to apply Subject-Aux Inversion. Is there any element in the PM in (79) that satisfies the SA of this transformation? Yes, the string *NP C M sleep* satisfies one case of the SA, (74b): *NP – C + M – X*. Applying the rule, we get the PM in (80).

(80)

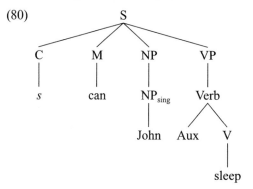

Now, can we apply Affix Hopping? Yes, and we get the PM in (81), where *s* has hopped onto M.

(81)

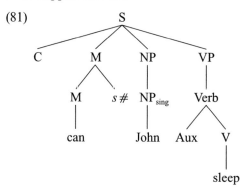

■ *Gutiérrez:*   When we apply Subject-Aux Inversion, we end up with Aux as a terminal symbol, but Aux isn't a terminal symbol.

Lasnik: It depends on what we mean by terminal symbol. The core notion of terminal versus nonterminal is relevant to the phrase structure grammar. The terminals have a particular role there, one they don't have in transformational derivations. When you're doing a phrase structure derivation and all you have left are terminal symbols, then you know the derivation is done. There's no analogous notion within transformational grammar, so although what you're saying is correct in a sense, it's not obviously of consequence.

In the mid '60s linguists did worry about this question. It's not that they had any clear evidence or argument, they just worried about it. A whole theory developed of what was called *tree pruning*, which was almost entirely intended to deal with the type of case we're discussing: if we have a nonterminal symbol that's resulted from transformational applications and that's come not to dominate anything, then we get rid of it by "pruning" that branch of the tree. We're going to assume that there's no such operation as tree pruning. If we find evidence that Aux is literally no longer there, then we'll try to build up a theory of tree pruning of our own.   ■

Finally, let's turn to the pair in (70), the most interesting of all: *John slept* and *Did John sleep?* The relevant initial PM is (82).

(82)

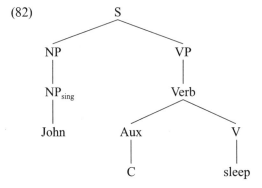

After we apply the Number Transformation, we have the derived PM in (83).

(83)

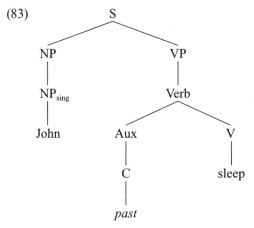

Let's see if we can apply Subject-Aux Inversion. Does anything in the derived PM (83) satisfy its SA? One element does, namely, *NP C V*, which satisfies the SA (74a), *NP – C – V X*. The rule can therefore apply, producing the derived PM (84).

(84)

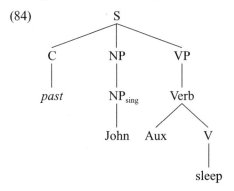

Can we now apply Affix Hopping to the PM in (84)? No, since *past* and V aren't adjacent; *John* intervenes between them. Thus, there's no element that satisfies the SA of Affix Hopping. Affix Hopping is obligatory, but it's obligatory in the sense we discussed earlier: we have to apply it *if we can*, but if we can't, we needn't. If the derivation stopped here, we would have *past John sleep* as our terminal string, an overgeneration problem.

The immediate adjacency requirement in Affix Hopping in fact represents an important generalization. In theories of syntax since about the late '60s, it's been impossible to say this, because everyone has argued or assumed that syntax never cares about adjacency. Consequently, as we'll see, no one now has a completely effective way to rule out *John not left*. In Lasnik 1995 I've argued that *Syntactic Structures* was right and that the modern theories of syntax are wrong in this regard (see section 3.8).

Regarding (84), Chomsky's insight was this. *Past John sleep* isn't a sentence of English, but it's very similar to *Did John sleep? Did* carries the information that the sentence is past tense, but it has no other semantic import; it's a pleonastic verb. We can say that *do* is a morphophonemic entity that "supports" the stranded *past* affix.

2.5.3   The Word Boundary Transformation T21a and *Do*-Support T21b

The generalization then is that whenever Affix Hopping T20 fails to apply, *do* comes to the rescue. Chomsky therefore proposed two rules, the Word Boundary Transformation T21a and the *do* Transformation T21b (known as *Do*-Support) that have the effect of turning the *past* in (84) into the past tense of a pleonastic verb *do*.[13] Let's see what each rule does.

(85) *T21a Word Boundary Transformation (obligatory)*
      SA: X – Y (where X ≠ "v" or Y ≠ "Af")
      SC: $X_1 - X_2 \rightarrow X_1 - \# \ X_2$

(86) *T21b do Transformation* (Do-*Support*) *(obligatory)*
      SA: # – "Af"
      SC: $X_1 - X_2 \rightarrow X_1 - do + X_2$

The Word Boundary Transformation looks at a structure, and if the structure has certain properties, it puts in the symbol #. *Do*-Support looks at a structure, and if the structure has the symbol # in a certain position, it puts in *do*.

For Chomsky, the Word Boundary Transformation was part of a more general process. For Chomsky in *Syntactic Structures*, the syntax had to set the stage for the morphophonemics. Part of setting the stage is breaking things up into words. The morphophonemics cares about where the word boundaries are—and the Word Boundary Transformation puts them all in.

Although the Word Boundary Transformation doesn't just prepare the string for *Do*-Support, let's see first if it in fact succeeds in doing that. In our PM in (84), the Word Boundary Transformation is trying to put word boundaries designated as # (which can be regarded as a sort of terminal symbol) in the places shown in (87).

(87)

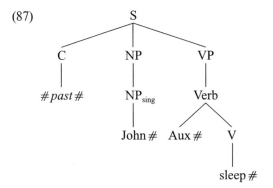

Then *Do*-Support will look at the result. *Do*-Support is trying to say, "When 'Af' immediately follows a word boundary, insert *do* there." The intention is that if and only if the affix has failed to hop, a # will be inserted in front of it. The technical problem is that neither the Word Boundary Transformation nor *Do*-Support is stated quite correctly in *Syntactic Structures*, so it's hard to see just how they work.

Let's fix *Do*-Support first because it's easier to fix. *Do*-Support is trying to say that when a word boundary is followed by an affix, the affix isn't part of a word, because Affix Hopping didn't work. Under that circumstance *Do*-Support applies.

Consider the SA of *Do*-Support, repeated here from (86).

(88) # – "Af"

As this SA is stated, *Do*-Support will apply only to a PM that consists of nothing except # and an immediately following "Af."[14] But there are no such PMs, either basic or derived. This is a trivial problem. We can fix it by inserting variables at the beginning and the end.

(89) *T21b Do-Support*
        SA: X – # – "Af" – Y

Now there are elements of the PM that satisfy the SA of *Do*-Support. One of them is *past NP VP*.

Now *Do*-Support can apply, changing the PM in some way. We can't tell just by looking at the SC of *Do*-Support in *Syntactic Structures* what Chomsky intended it to do. In *LSLT* he clarified this: *Do*-Support should left-adjoin *do* to "Af." What does this say? That *do* and *past* constitute a *past*. In other words, *did* is simply a past. Applying *Do*-Support to (87), we thus get the derived PM in (90).

(90)

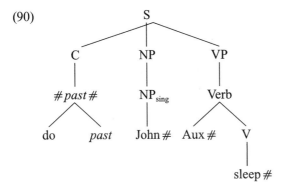

Now let's return to the problem with the statement of the Word Boundary Transformation. This transformation does two things: (1) it separates all the words in the PM; (2) it sets the stage for *Do*-Support, by picking out a stranded affix—in other words, by specifically homing in on an affix that hasn't hopped. If we have an affix that has hopped, we don't want it to trigger *Do*-Support. In fact, suppose we had an affix that did hop while we were trying to generate *John slept*, and we applied *Do*-Support. What would we get?

(91)

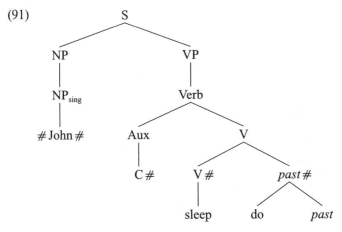

As (91) shows, we would get **John sleep did*. This is one of the problems with the Word Boundary Transformation as it is stated in *Syntactic Structures*, since it *does* incorrectly insert # between *sleep* and *past*, as we will see.

The Word Boundary Transformation obviously applies in many places in the structure, because it is intended to set off all the words with word boundaries. So we have to ask: Does it apply everywhere at once? Or does it iterate—and if so, does it work left to right, or right to left? Let's ignore these questions for the moment, and just focus on the relevant part of the tree. Specifically, we want the Word Boundary Transformation to put word boundaries everywhere *except* between *sleep* and *past* in (91), because, as just discussed, if it succeeded in putting a word boundary between *sleep* and *past*, then *Do*-Support would insert *do*, and we would incorrectly generate *John sleep did. Recall that the Word Boundary Transformation is obligatory; so wherever it can apply, it must apply. We therefore have to see if there's any way it can apply and put a word boundary between *sleep* and *past*. If it does, it will clearly yield an incorrect output, as well as prevent the correct output—a case of both overgeneration and undergeneration.

As stated in *Syntactic Structures* and shown in (85), the SA of the Word Boundary Transformation is as follows:

(92) *T21a Word Boundary Transformation*
      SA: X – Y (where X ≠ "v" or Y ≠ "Af")

Let's find out if there's any element of the PM in (91) that can be broken up so it satisfies X–Y and the requirement in parentheses. Consider the following element of the PM:

(93) $\underbrace{\text{John Aux V}}_{\text{X}}$ – $\underbrace{past}_{\text{Y}}$

Is the SA satisfied if *John Aux V* is X and *past* is Y? If so, the Word Boundary Transformation will incorrectly put a word boundary between *John Aux V* and *past*. Well, we can initially analyze *John Aux V* as X and *past* as Y. Does this analysis satisfy the requirement "X ≠ 'v' or Y ≠ 'Af' "? Let's first look at Y—here, *past*. Recall that "Af" isn't a symbol of the grammar, but an expression that Chomsky used to stand for *s, past, ∅, ing, en*. In reality, then, Y ≠ "Af" abbreviates five statements:

(94) Y ≠ *s*
      Y ≠ *past*
      Y ≠ ∅
      Y ≠ ing
      Y ≠ en

How are these five statements related: disjunctively or conjunctively? In fact, the requirement is *conjunctive*. The statement should look like this:

(95) Y ≠ *s* &
    Y ≠ *past* &
    Y ≠ ∅ &
    Y ≠ ing &
    Y ≠ en

The idea is that Y should not be any "Af" at all. In our example Y = *past*, so Y ≠ "Af" doesn't hold. We haven't satisfied that part of the requirement in the SA of the Word Boundary Transformation. This is good, because we don't want this rule to apply here.

But now let's look at the first part of the requirement, X ≠ "v," since in order for (93) to satisfy the SA of the Word Boundary Transformation, it will suffice that the requirement on X be satisfied (remember the disjunctive *or* in this statement). What does X ≠ "v" mean? It means the following:

(96) X ≠ M &
    X ≠ have &
    X ≠ be &
    X ≠ V

Recall that our X is *John Aux V*. Obviously, this X ≠ "v," so the requirement *is* satisfied, and this means that the PM in (91) satisfies the SA of the Word Boundary Transformation. We must therefore apply the rule, since it is obligatory, and we will (contrary to our initial intention) put a word boundary between *John Aux V* and *past*. *Do*-Support will apply, and we will incorrectly generate *John sleep did (and incorrectly fail to generate *John slept*, an instance of overgeneration and undergeneration). Clearly, the statement of the rule must be corrected.

What we really want to do is to divide the string into two parts such that the first part doesn't *end* with a verb, or the second part doesn't *begin* with an affix, a stronger requirement than the one in the *Syntactic Structures* statement (though surely what Chomsky actually intended). The modified SA for the Word Boundary Transformation will look like this:

(97) *T21a Word Boundary Transformation*
    SA (revised): X – Y (where X ≠ Z "v" or Y ≠ "Af" W)[15]

Let's see if this will give the correct result for the element in (93) that we were discussing, where X = *John Aux V* and Y = *past*. Notice that X ends in a "v," so the X requirement isn't satisfied. And Y begins with an "Af," so the Y requirement isn't satisfied either. We correctly predict that the rule won't apply here.

However, let's look at another element of the PM in (91): *John Aux sleep past*, where *X = John Aux sleep* and *Y = past*. Does the new Y satisfy the requirement? No, it doesn't; the new Y is the old Y, so it begins with an "Af." Does the new X satisfy the requirement? Unfortunately, it does. X (*John Aux sleep*) doesn't end in a "v" (namely, *have, be*, M, or V). True, *sleep* bears the "is a" relation to V, but the symbol *sleep* is not the symbol V. In the formulation of *LSLT* and *Syntactic Structures*, this is a fundamental distinction. So we still have a problem. The rule will incorrectly apply and we will overgenerate *John sleep did (and, as before, fail to generate *John left*). Strangely, it's not enough, in this case, to find one element of the PM that satisfies the SA. We'll deal with this thorny problem a bit later (see section 2.6.2.1).

We saw that Affix Hopping fails when the affix and the verb aren't adjacent to each other, and that this happens when we've previously applied Subject-Aux Inversion. Another way an affix can be separated from its verb is through the Negation Transformation (T16), to which I now turn.

2.5.4   Negation Transformation T16

Chomsky formulated T_{not}, the Negation Transformation T16, as follows:

(98) *T16 Negation Transformation (optional)*
      SA: a. NP – C – V X
          b. NP – C + M – X
          c. NP – C + have – X
          d. NP – C + be – X
      SC: $X_1 - X_2 - X_3 \rightarrow X_1 - X_2 + $ n't $ - X_3$

First of all, notice that the Negation Transformation has the same SA as both Affirmation T17 and Subject-Aux Inversion T18. All three SAs partition the structure in the same way. Chomsky regarded it as a significant generalization that all three transformations have the same SA. It isn't obvious, though, that if we have to state the same SA in separate rules, we've truly *captured* the generalization. That's something we'll do later. We'll see how a principled modification of these processes allows us to factor that generalization out so we don't have to state it as part of several separate rules.

The Negation Transformation is responsible for sentences like (99).

(99) John can't swim

As we know, a transformation does two things: it checks to see whether the current PM is eligible, and if so, alters it in some fashion. Let's trace a derivation of (99) through the Number Transformation T15 and then see how the Negation Transformation might analyze and affect the derived PM.

(100) shows the graphic representation of the initial PM.

(100)
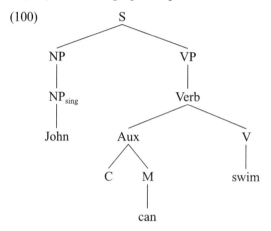

Now we apply the Number Transformation, and we "rewrite" C as the abstract morpheme *s*.

(101)
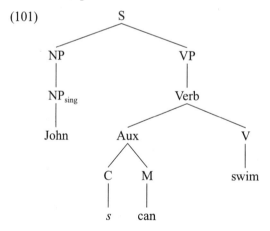

Now we're ready for the Negation Transformation. We want to see if there's an element of the PM in (101) that satisfies the SA (98b) and qualifies the rule to apply. There are in fact two such elements, shown in (102).

(98)   b. NP – C + M – X

(102) a. NP C M V

     b. NP C M swim

Let's look at the string (102a). This string has three parts, as far as the Negation Transformation is concerned: NP, C followed by M, and V (which satisfies the variable).

(103) NP – C + M – V

We need to know several things in order to see what the Negation Transformation is going to do, and none of them are transparent in the presentation of the rule in *Syntactic Structures*. One thing we need to know is what operation the rule carries out. Well, we know it's some kind of insertion, because there's no *n't* in the input, and the output is supposed to have *n't* in it. But just knowing that *n't* is inserted doesn't necessarily tell us *how* it's inserted. We have to know that the intended operation is *adjunction*. Unfortunately, adjunction isn't well defined for what we're trying to do here. Chomsky intended *n't* to adjoin to the second term of the SA. Now, we know what it means to adjoin one category to another or a morpheme to a category (see section 2.3.2.1), but we don't know what it means to adjoin to a *sequence* C-followed-by-M; that isn't a well-defined operation. The second term of the analysis is *C M*, crucially not *Aux*, as we will see momentarily.

So, we will just stipulate that right-adjoining to a term of an SA that consists of two symbols means right-adjoining to the rightmost one. (Symmetrically, left-adjoining to a sequence of two symbols will mean left-adjoining to the leftmost one.) This will give us the derived PM in (104).

(104)

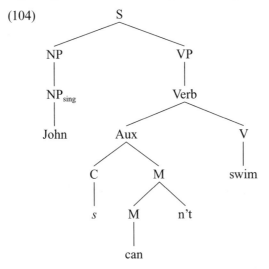

Why don't we get rid of the whole problem by saying that what the rule does is right-adjoin *n't* to Aux? Because then we would predict that *n't* would always wind up at the end of the auxiliary sequence, whereas the true generalization is that *n't* always comes after the *first* auxiliary verb.

Notice that this is the same type of generalization that holds for Subject-Aux Inversion. Subject-Aux Inversion doesn't invert the whole Aux with the subject; instead, it inverts the first auxiliary verb with the subject, and the morpheme that will go with it, always a C morpheme.

So, neither the Negation Transformation nor Subject-Aux Inversion involves the whole item Aux; they both involve the first auxiliary verb. In the case we're discussing, (104), it's hard to tell that this is what's happening, because the example has only one auxiliary verb. But if we add more auxiliary verbs, we can clearly see the difference.

(105)   John mustn't have been swimming

(106)   *John must have beenn't swimming
       (*or* *John must have been doing n't swim)

To recap: There are two things we needed to know that weren't explicit in the presentation in *Syntactic Structures*: (1) that the operation Chomsky had in mind for the Negation Transformation is adjunction, and (2) how to interpret adjunction, a binary process defined on two symbols, when one symbol needs to be adjoined to a sequence of two symbols. We stipulated that interpretation: right adjunction right-adjoins to the rightmost symbol; left adjunction left-adjoins to the leftmost symbol.

We still have to integrate the contents of C with the M constituent in (104). That is, Affix Hopping T20 has to apply. We know that it has to apply, because if it were prevented from applying, we would end up with a sentence like (107).

(107)   *John does can't swim

Here, the "stranded" *s* has triggered *Do*-Support. To apply Affix Hopping, we have to find an element in the (further derived)[16] PM in (104) that satisfies its SA, repeated here:[17]

(108)   *T20 Affix Hopping*
       SA: X – "Af" – "v" – Y

Two elements in (104) that satisfy the SA of Affix Hopping are shown in (109).

(109)   a. John *s* M swim
       b. John *s* M n't swim

If we choose the element (109a) of the PM to satisfy the SA of Affix Hopping, then we will analyze the structure in the following way:

(110) John   *s*   M   swim
          X – "Af" – "v" – Y

If, on the other hand, we choose the element (109b), we will analyze the structure in the following way:

(111) John   *s*   M   n't swim
          X – "Af" – "v" –   Y

Depending on what element we choose, Affix Hopping will result in one or the other of two different structures. If we choose element (109a), we'll end up with the structure in (112a), whereas if we choose element (109b), we'll end up with the one in (112b).

(112) a.

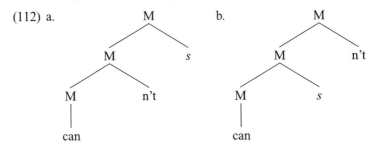

(112a) and (112b) are two different formal objects. However, they might not be *relevantly* different formal objects. That is, if no semantic, syntactic, or phonological rule distinguishes them, then the difference is one that doesn't really matter. But one could imagine that some rule would distinguish them, and then we'd have to make a decision.

There are two choices: either stipulate something that could distinguish between these objects, or just allow both of them. The only way to decide which approach is right is to see if any other process in the grammar makes the distinction. In fact, shortly after *Syntactic Structures* appeared, in the very early '60s, Chomsky explored other phenomena that raised similar questions, and he proposed a principle of grammar that would require taking the analysis in (112a). He called it the *A-over-A Constraint*. This constraint said that if a transformation is about to apply to a PM, and it applies ambiguously both to one thing of category A and to another thing of category A dominated by the first thing of category A, it has to pick the higher one (the A that is "over" the other A). What Chomsky was concerned with then were cases where an NP is embedded inside another

NP. In such cases Chomsky observed that many operations that do something to an NP will only do it to the one that's higher. Trying to apply the operation to the embedded NP gives a bad result. One possible case of this, discussed in great detail by Ross (1967), involves examples like these:

(113)   John and Mary, I like

(114)   *Mary, I like John and

Here we see that if Topicalization applies, it can move the "bigger" NP *Mary and John*, giving the acceptable result in (113), but if it moves the "smaller" NP *Mary* (which was part of the bigger NP), the resulting structure in (114) is bad.

Thus, if the A-over-A Constraint is taken in a totally general way and if we anachronistically apply it to the analyses in (112a) and (112b), then we have to conclude that (112a) is the correct analysis.

▪ *Vukić:*   The problem with that is that (112b) more closely mirrors the morphological structure of the word.

Lasnik: Yes, I share your intuition. So keep this possible contradiction in mind. To clearly decide which analysis is correct, though, we need to find some syntactic, phonological, or semantic process that applies differentially to (112a) and (112b) and that gives a good result for one and a bad result for the other. We can't just rely on our theoretical intuitions.   ▪

We've looked at one instance of the Negation Transformation, with a modal. Let's look at two more instances, one involving auxiliary *be*, and one lacking an auxiliary verb altogether and thus requiring an application of *Do*-Support.

We'll start with virtually the same PM as (100), but instead of deriving *John can't swim* we'll derive *John isn't swimming*.

(115)

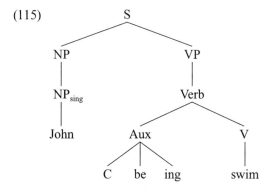

We begin with the PM of which (115) is a graphic representation. Then, as usual, we apply the Number Transformation, ending up in this case with (116).

(116)

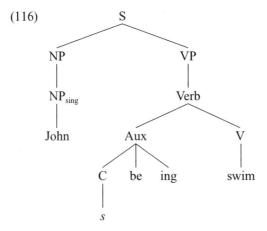

Immediately, we can see another reason why we can't adjoin *n't* to the end of Aux. If we did, then *ing* wouldn't be adjacent to the verb, and we wouldn't be able to apply Affix Hopping. The result would be something like this:

(117) *John is doing n't swim

Now, we have to ask the usual two questions: Does the Negation Transformation have a relevant SA, one that has a chance of being satisfied? And, is there an element in the derived PM of which (116) is a graphic representation that satisfies that SA?

It appears that the SA of the Negation Transformation in (98d), repeated here, has a chance of being satisfied.

(98) d. NP – C + be – X

The following two elements of the PM in (116) can satisfy this SA:

(118) a. NP C be ing swim
       b. NP C be ing V

Therefore, the Negation Transformation is eligible to apply; so let's apply it. First the rule analyzes the structure into three parts.

(119) NP – C + be – ing swim
       or
       NP – C + be – ing V

Then it right-adjoins *n't* to the second term (both cases must give the same result this time). Recall that in *Syntactic Structures* this wasn't a well-defined operation; we made it well defined by specifying that it right-adjoins *n't* to the rightmost element of the second term. Right adjunction to *be* is somewhat peculiar too, but we already encountered that peculiarity when we considered Affix Hopping onto *be*. When we hop an affix onto *be*, we're creating another thing that we're also calling *be*. Though it seemed strange, we had to regard *be* as a sort of simultaneously abstract and concrete entity, both a category label and the contents of the category. So the Negation Transformation will apply in the current case, right-adjoining *n't* to *be* and resulting in the PM in (120).

(120)

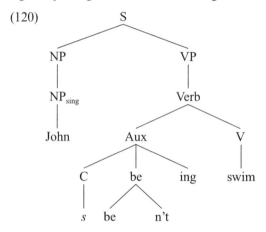

We still have to apply Affix Hopping. The same ambiguity of application turns up here as in the earlier example. Affix Hopping will look for something like *s* and for something like *be*. But there are two different occurrences of *be* immediately after *s*: the higher one and the lower one. So, in accord with what we said above, either Affix Hopping has two different outputs, or we have to add some principle to the theory of grammar that says that in this kind of case a transformation will always choose one or the other, perhaps the A-over-A Constraint.[18] As the theory stands right now, there are two possibilities: we can adjoin *s* either to the higher *be* or to the lower *be* in (120), resulting in two different objects, (121a) and (121b).

(121) a.   b.

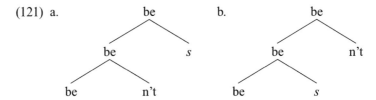

Again, it might perfectly well be that neither the semantics nor the morphophonemics will care which of those two objects we end up with.

Finally, let's look at the case where the initial PM has no auxiliary
verbs at all. In this case we ultimately want to generate the sentence *John
doesn't swim*. Let's start with the PM in (122).

(122)

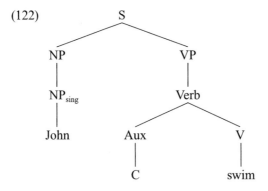

As usual, we apply the Number Transformation, in this case obtaining the
PM (123).

(123)

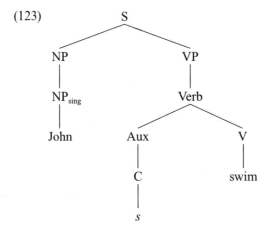

Now we're ready to apply the Negation Transformation. Does one of its SAs have a chance of being satisfied? SA (98a) does. Further, only one element in the PM in (123) satisfies this SA.

(98)   a. NP – C – V X

(124)   NP C V

We therefore analyze this element into three parts.

(125) NP – C – V

This is the first instance of the Negation Transformation we've looked at where the basic operation of adjunction is perfectly well defined. The second term in (125) consists of exactly one symbol, and we know how to right-adjoin a symbol to a symbol. Applying the transformation results in the PM in (126).

(126)

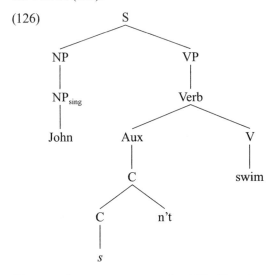

Next, we have to try to apply Affix Hopping. Recall that Chomsky formulated the SA of Affix Hopping as follows:

(127) *T20 Affix Hopping*
      SA: X – "Af" – "v" – Y (where "Af" is any C or *en* or *ing*;
          "v" is any M or V or *have* or *be*)

But we know from (50), repeated here, that this SA actually designates a group of expressions.

$$(50)\quad X - \begin{Bmatrix} s \\ past \\ \varnothing \\ en \\ ing \end{Bmatrix} - \begin{Bmatrix} V \\ M \\ have \\ be \end{Bmatrix} - Y$$

In other words, the SA of Affix Hopping is really an abbreviation of 20 different SAs. We can easily see now that Affix Hopping can't apply here because *s* isn't adjacent to V: *n't* is in the way. Now, it's important to see that the phrase *any* C in the parenthetical part of Affix Hopping's SA is potentially misleading. If we say that C is *itself* the relevant element, then when we look at the PM in (126), we end up applying Affix Hopping and we incorrectly generate (128), since we adjoin the whole element C, including the adjoined *n't*, to the verb.

(128) *John swimsn't

Thus, *any* C means *s*, $\varnothing$, or *past*, but not the symbol C itself. We must therefore avoid the temptation to collapse the second term of (50) in the following way (which seemingly reduces the number of SAs from 20 to 12):

$$(129)\quad \begin{Bmatrix} C \\ en \\ ing \end{Bmatrix}$$

This same example shows why Chomsky didn't want *n't* to adjoin to *s*, but did want *n't* to adjoin to C. If *n't* adjoined to *s*, we would have a similar problem: the *s* with the *n't* adjoined to it would hop onto the verb and we would again get the ungrammatical sentence (128). So, this one bad example shows us two significant details about the system: (1) the sort of complication in Affix Hopping we've just been looking at, and (2) why the Negation Transformation has to adjoin *n't* to C and not to *s*.

We've kept Affix Hopping from applying in (126), but we aren't done yet. We've had a particular intuition about how the system hangs together. Whenever we keep Affix Hopping from applying, various other things ultimately result in an application of *Do*-Support. One thing that happens is the Word Boundary Transformation T21a; in particular, it puts a boundary right before the *s* in (126), producing the PM in (130).

(130)

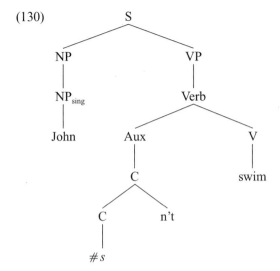

The next transformation, *Do*-Support T21b, will notice that there's an affix *s* immediately preceded by a word boundary, and it will adjoin *do* to that affix. We end up with the PM of which (131) is a graphic representation.

(131)

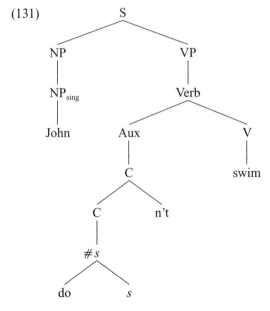

- *Gutiérrez:* Won't the Word Boundary Transformation put a word boundary before *n't*?

Lasnik: Yes, it will put a word boundary there (and in several other places as well). Though it seems rather counterintuitive, as far as this system is concerned this would have no undesirable effects, because *n't* isn't an "Af" and there's no danger that *Do*-Support will apply an extra time. The only relevant work the Word Boundary Transformation does here is marking off an affix that hasn't hopped. *n't* is a sort of clitic (a word that's become affixlike), but it isn't one of the five things that Chomsky means by "Af" namely, *s, past,* $\emptyset$, *en,* and *ing.* ∎

2.5.5 Affirmation (T17)

Let's take a brief look at T17 (Chomsky's T_A, which we can call *Affirmation*) and the motivations behind it. In *Syntactic Structures* Chomsky stated Affirmation as follows (p. 112):

(132) *T17 Affirmation (optional)*
       SA: same as the Negation Transformation T16
       SC: $X_1 - X_2 - X_3 \rightarrow X_1 - X_2 + A - X_3$

Affirmation is identical to the Negation Transformation except that instead of inserting a marker of negation into the structure, it inserts a marker of strong affirmation, one that has the effect of heavy stress.

(133) a. John IS swimming (with stress on *is*)
       b. John CAN swim (with stress on *can*)
       c. John DOES swim (with stress on *does*)

The generalization that Chomsky had in mind is that in this kind of affirmation, it's the first auxiliary verb that gets heavy stress, if there *is* an auxiliary verb; otherwise, *do* is inserted and gets heavy stress. The *A* in the SC is a morpheme just like *n't*, and if it's inserted between an affix and a verb, it blocks Affix Hopping T20, because it blocks adjacency. *A* is a formal symbol of the grammar. Affirmation is thus exactly like the Negation Transformation except that the morpheme that's inserted can't be identified segmentally, but only by extra extra heavy stress on the word bearing the *A*.

2.5.6 Interaction between the Negation Transformation T16 and Subject-Auxiliary Inversion T18

In this section we will investigate the interesting question of how the Negation Transformation T16 and Subject-Aux Inversion T18 may interact.

2.5.6.1 Negative Questions

Imagine a PM to which we've applied the Number Transformation T15 and then the Negation Transformation T16. Now, is it possible to apply Subject-Aux Inversion T18, and if so, what do we get? Specifically, let's look at the derived PM in (134).

(134)

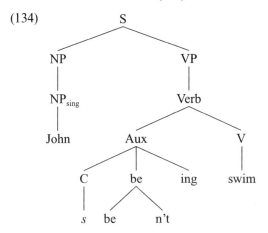

One element that satisfies the SA of Subject-Aux Inversion is the following:

(135) NP C be ing swim

This element satisfies the SA in (74d).

(74) d. NP – C + be – X

Subject-Aux Inversion will permute the first term and the second term. Recall that in a case like this we need a special notion of permutation. Permuting NP and VP would be like rotating a mobile, but permuting NP and C + *be* isn't quite like that. The result of applying Subject-Aux Inversion, according to Chomsky, would be the PM in (136).

(136)

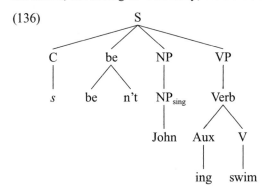

Next we need to do two familiar things. We have to hop *ing* onto *swim*; and we have to hop *s* onto *be*, which is mildly complicated because *be* is now a more complex item. But this isn't a new problem; we would have had to do it even if we hadn't applied Subject-Aux Inversion. The affix *s* has to hop onto the complex *be*, and the whole item has to be interpreted by the morphophonemics as *isn't*.

Now we have a perfectly good way of generating *Isn't John swimming?* That's a virtue of the system: once we have the Negation Transformation and Subject-Aux Inversion, we don't need a special transformation to derive negative questions. We get them for free. Transformational theory has come so far that it's hard to remember when a result like that was a really powerful argument for looking at things a certain way. Nowadays transformations are mostly so general that you cannot see such inter-actions between transformations; but back then, when they were so specific, it was a real accomplishment if two specific transformations devoted to two specific kinds of sentences would interact to generate a third kind of sentence, as they do here.[19]

Now, let's "undo" Subject-Aux Inversion and ask if there's another element of the PM in (134) that would satisfy its SA in (74d) in a different way. In fact, there is one, shown here in (137a) and analyzed as (137b).

(74)   d.   NP – C + be – X

(137) a.   NP C be n't ing swim
       b.   NP – C be – n't ing swim

Given this analysis, we would end up with the PM in (138) when Subject-Aux Inversion applies.

(138)

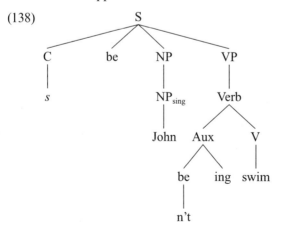

After Affix Hopping, we would end up with the completely ungrammatical sentence (139).

(139) *Is John n't swimming?

There are two things wrong with this analysis—one clearly, the other intuitively. The thing that's clearly wrong is that (139) is a wildly ungrammatical sentence. The intuition is that *n't* isn't an instance of *be*, though the PM in (138) makes it look like that. Note that the A-over-A Constraint, a later development, would prevent this derivation. The PM in (134) has two occurrences of *be*. If we're allowed to move the lower *be*, there are two possible results, one good and one bad. If we were required to move the lower *be*, we would only derive the bad sentence, and we wouldn't derive the good sentence at all. By contrast, the A-over-A Constraint would force us to apply Subject-Aux Inversion to the higher *be*, deriving only the good sentence. Hence, it looks like the A-over-A Constraint is motivated even in this theory, and our intuition about preferring a structure that more closely mirrors the morphology (see Vukić's remark above) is wrong. Is that a big problem? Not necessarily. What this depends on is exactly what the path between syntax and morphophonemics is like. If that path is totally transparent, then this result might be a problem, but if what Chomsky and Halle (1968) called *readjustment rules* from the syntax to the morphophonemics do exist, then it isn't necessarily a problem at all.

■ *Gutiérrez:*   How about the semantics? We end up with the structure in (140).

(140)

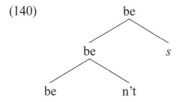

Here, it looks like only *be* is negated; *s* isn't.

Lasnik: That's an excellent question. A lot of modern theories assume that structure transparently represents scope relations (see May 1977). The problem is that the whole theory breaks down for auxiliaries and negation. For instance, the scope properties of a modal with respect to negation don't seem to be predictable from its morphology. Let me show you what I mean.

Look at the following contrast:

(141) You mustn't leave

(142) You needn't leave

In (141) the negation is semantically "lower" than the necessity. (141) means that it's necessary that you not leave. It doesn't mean that it's not necessary that you leave. However, (142) has parallel morphology but the meaning is reversed. (142) means that it isn't necessary that you leave. It doesn't mean that it's necessary that you not leave. So, exactly in this fragment of grammar, all theories of how structure and scope interact collapse, a problem that has been recognized for at least 30 years. I've never seen a complete solution to it.

Ultimately, your question is very important. I've hinted at how the syntax interacts with the morphophonemics in this theory. We apply the PS rules, we apply transformations, and then we do the morphophonemics. I haven't talked at all about how any of this interacts with the semantics. Chomsky proposed that it interacts with the semantics in exactly the same way it interacts with the morphophonemics. We apply the PS rules and the transformations, and the resulting structure feeds into the semantics. It's important to know what the final structure is, in order to know what the meaning is. However, for auxiliary verbs and negation no one seems to have a workable theory. ■

2.5.6.2 *Do*-Support T21b
Now let's look at how *Do*-Support T21b interacts with the Negation Transformation T16 and Subject-Aux Inversion T18. We'll start with the derived PM in (126), repeated here, after the application of the Number Transformation T15 and the Negation Transformation.

(126)

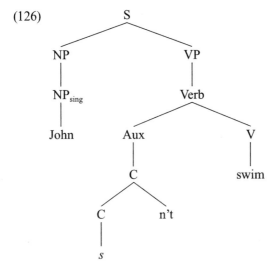

Now we can apply Subject-Aux Inversion, deriving the PM in (143).

(143)

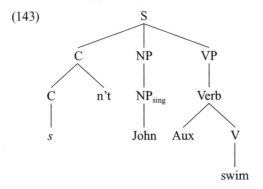

We can't apply Affix Hopping T20 because the affix *s* and the V are no longer adjacent. So we apply the Word Boundary Transformation T21a, with the result shown in (144).

(144)

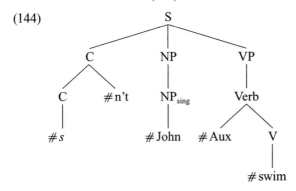

We now apply *Do*-Support, and we end up with the PM in (145) (abstracting away from #s).

(145)

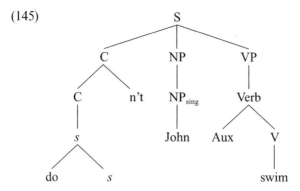

In this way we're able to generate *Doesn't John swim?* with no new machinery at all.

2.5.7   Summary

We've talked about the motivations for transformations: relatedness between sentences, cross-serial dependencies, things that PS rules can't handle.

We've looked at the Number Transformation T15. The Number Transformation stands out among the transformations because it looks so much like a PS rule. On the other hand, if we grouped it with the PS rules, it would stand out there too. That's because the PS component in this theory consists of context-free rewriting rules, and the Number Transformation is context sensitive.

We've also looked at Affix Hopping T20. Affix Hopping has the effect of taking an "Af" (not a term in the grammar) and a "v" (a "little v," not a term in the grammar either), which are independent syntactically, and associating the "Af" with the "v." It puts them together into what the morphophonemics will see as a word.

There are circumstances where Affix Hopping can't apply. The SA of Affix Hopping makes some formally true statements. It doesn't matter what's at the beginning of the sentence (X). It doesn't matter what's at the end of the sentence (Y). It *does* matter that "Af" and "v" are adjacent to each other.

(146) *T20 Affix Hopping*
       SA: X – "Af" – "v" – Y

When a PM contains an "Af" and a "v" but they aren't adjacent, Affix Hopping doesn't apply. Affix Hopping is an obligatory rule, but remember what "obligatory" means in this system: if the SA is satisfied, we have to apply the rule, but if we can't apply it, we don't have to.

How could a situation ever arise where "Af" and "v" aren't adjacent to each other? Not by the PS rules in this system. But there are transformations that can cause this situation. One of them is Subject-Aux Inversion T18, which has the effect of taking some element and moving it to the front of the sentence. Sometimes, when that happens, an affix gets separated from the verb it would like to hop onto. Another such transformation is the Negation Transformation T16, which introduces *n't* into the structure. Sometimes it's introduced in such a way that it separates an affix and the verb it would like to hop onto. Affirmation T17 works the same way.

Here's the big generalization:

(147) When Affix Hopping fails, a pleonastic (semantically empty) verb *do* is inserted to support the stranded "Af."

Do-Support T21b is the transformation that introduces *do*.

Exercises

1. In tree form, present a PM to which the Passive Transformation T12 could apply, and present one to which it could not apply. For the PM that "fits" the rule, display a member of the set-theoretic PM that establishes the PM's eligibility to undergo the rule.

2. Present an argument that *be* must never be a V. That is, show that something would go empirically wrong if *be* were ever introduced by a rule such as V → *be*. (Is the problem overgeneration, undergeneration, or both?) [Note that I'm not asking whether the *Syntactic Structures* rules as they're stated introduce *be* under V. I know that you know that they don't. Rather, I'm asking why the rules couldn't be changed so as to (sometimes) make *be* a V, *especially when it seems to be the "main verb" of the sentence*.]

3. Show precisely why Subject-Aux Inversion T18 is ordered before Affix Hopping T20. What would go wrong if Affix Hopping (as stated in *Syntactic Structures*) were ordered before Subject-Aux Inversion (as stated in *Syntactic Structures*)? What would go wrong if these two rules were unordered (i.e., freely ordered) with respect to each other? Be explicit.

4. The present plural morpheme for regular verbs is phonetically null. Demonstrate empirically that there really is a morpheme introduced under C in these

cases, rather than nothing at all. That is, show some incorrect prediction that would be made otherwise.

5. Show precisely how each of the following ungrammatical examples is ruled out. Or, to put the same question another way, for each example, state the minimal change in the grammar that would allow it to be generated.
a. *Does John have left? (cf. Has John left?)
b. *John *past* win the race (cf. John won the race)
c. *Saw Susan the man? (cf. Did Susan see the man?)
d. *Mary likesn't Bill (cf. Mary doesn't like Bill)

6. [In this exercise, don't use any examples you've discussed in other exercises in this group. Come up with new examples. In fact, try hard to come up with new types of examples.]

A. Present an unacceptable sentence that can be generated by the rules in *Syntactic Structures* as modified in this chapter, and show how the sentence is generated. [You don't have to give a complete derivation—just enough to make it clear what's going on.] Briefly discuss what the deficiency in the system seems to be.

B. Present an acceptable sentence that can't be generated by the rules in *Syntactic Structures* as modified in this chapter, and show why it can't be generated. Briefly discuss what the deficiency in the system seems to be.

2.6 THEORETICAL ISSUES RAISED BY *SYNTACTIC STRUCTURES*

The transformations we've been looking at presuppose a particular *theory* of transformations, one that makes claims about what a possible transformation is. In some respects the theory makes too many possibilities available. Let's examine this issue.

2.6.1 Terms and Constituent Structure

First let's consider what a term in a structural analysis can be.

Recall our definition from (14) of section 2.3.1.1. A term can be

• Any sequence of symbols (terminals, nonterminals, and variables) *or*
• A set of sequences of symbols *or*
• A Boolean combination of these

There's an objection to be raised about the option of defining a term as a *sequence* of symbols. This possibility seems to undermine one of the major insights of transformational generative grammar. Chomsky has always argued that the best way to determine the constituent structure of a sequence of words is to apply transformations to it—this will reveal where the constituent breaks are. Behind this claim is the intuition that the terms of an SA have to be constituents. However, that's only true if we limit the definition of *term* to (13a–c). If we allow a term to be a sequence of symbols, then we're saying that any two things can move around as a unit as long as they happen to be next to each other, or any 17 things can move around as long as they happen to be next to each other. They don't have to constitute a constituent; they don't have to be "a branch in the tree." We saw an example of this when we applied Subject-Aux Inversion T18 and moved *s* and *be* to the front of the PM, even though they don't constitute a constituent. If Chomsky's intuition and argument that transformations provide the most reliable test for constituent structure are right, then we have to get rid of the part of the definition of *term* involving sequence of symbols.

2.6.2   Boolean and Quantificational Conditions

In *Aspects* Chomsky argued that including quantificational conditions in SAs would give transformations too much descriptive power, and that SAs should be limited to Boolean conditions. We will consider the *Syntactic Structures* theory in this light.

2.6.2.1   Negation, Conjunction, and Disjunction in Structural Analyses

Surprisingly, it turns out that an SA involving negative requirements ($\neq$) of the type found, for instance, in the Word Boundary Transformation T21a, fails to have a crucial property that Chomsky, in *Aspects*, claimed SAs must have—namely, that an SA is a *Boolean condition on analyzability*. (A Boolean condition is a condition stated in terms of the propositional connectives: Boolean *and*, Boolean *or*, Boolean *not*, Boolean *if...then*.) Chomsky contrasted that claim with one he rejected: that an SA can be a *quantificational* statement.

In *Aspects* Chomsky posed the question, should transformations be allowed to be quantificational statements? His answer was no—allowing this would give transformations too much power, it would permit too wide a variety of transformations and grammars and thereby make the acquisition problem insurmountable. Given all the quantificational statements there can be, there would be no way for the learner to arrive at the right solution to the acquisition problem. Therefore, Chomsky said, we will limit the theory of grammar, so that learners will never even consider a quantificational statement in a rule. They will be limited to Boolean statements only.

The logic of that argument is impeccable. Unfortunately, the facts are very recalcitrant, because one of the classic Boolean conditions Chomsky almost certainly had in mind is negation ($\neq$), as in the rule we were just looking at (the Word Boundary Transformation T21a). But this negation isn't Boolean; it's in fact quantificational. It has an implicit universal quantifier in it. We have to interpret it as meaning that it's not enough to find *some* element of the PM that satisfies the condition; rather, *all* the relevant elements must satisfy it. All uses of *not* in transformations of the '50s and '60s are quantificational in this way, as I will now show.

Certainly, no sane linguist would ever propose an SA that will be satisfied if there's some way of analyzing the structure in question such that some symbol is simply *not* some other symbol. That condition can virtually always be satisfied. If the prohibited symbol is V, then we can use *swim*. If the prohibited symbol is *swim*, then we can use V. No one ever proposed an SA that really uses Boolean negation; all SAs have used quantificational negation. So, if we need negation at all, the version we need is quantificational. Thus, given Chomsky's *Aspects* argument, we hope we don't need negation at all.

We would hope to be able to follow some version of the approach that Chomsky took in *Aspects* to dispense with the one quantificational condition he explicitly considered. Chomsky was concerned with the phenomenon of "deletion under identity," where some constituent is deleted if it's identical to another constituent. VP-deletion is a standard case.

(148) Mary will solve the problem and John will ~~solve the problem~~ too

The question is how to characterize identity. Obviously, identity of category isn't sufficient. Just being a VP isn't enough for the second VP to be deleted "under identity" with the first. And identity of terminal string doesn't suffice. The string has to be a VP. Finally, identity of category (VP in this case) *and* of terminal string doesn't always suffice either. If the VPs display a structural ambiguity, it has to be resolved the same way in both VPs. Thus, the identity condition relies on a universal quantifier: the two VPs must be identical with respect to *every* element of their (sub) PMs. To avoid allowing such a powerful descriptive device in particular transformations, Chomsky proposed that the relevant notion of identity isn't part of any transformation. Instead, he proposed, it is factored out of particular rules, and out of particular grammars, and is stated once and for all in Universal Grammar; this is the condition of *recoverability of deletion.* This solution entails, apparently correctly, that the relevant notion of identity is common across languages. On this model, we would hope to likewise capture the effects of quantificational negation by some property of Universal Grammar.

As for Boolean negation, one can, of course, allow it into the theory if one wants to, but it's never going to do any work. Stating transformations in terms of Boolean negation will virtually never prevent a rule from applying, but negation in an SA is supposed to do exactly that. It imposes a requirement on what PMs are eligible to undergo the transformation.

Let's consider other Boolean conditions. How about Boolean *disjunction (or)*? This condition is descriptively very useful, for example, in the Negation Transformation T16, whose SA in (74) is repeated here. (Recall that this is also the SA for Affirmation T17 and Subject-Aux Inversion T18.)

(74) *T16 Negation Transformation (optional)*
     SA: a. NP – C – V X
         b. NP – C + M – X
         c. NP – C + have – X
         d. NP – C + be – X

Boolean disjunction is very popular. We seem to be stuck with it at the moment, but there is, and always was, a huge objection to it, namely, Ross's objection (see section 2.5.1). This objection is a very powerful one, equal in importance to Chomsky's rejection of quantificational conditions in SAs. Boolean *or* allows vast descriptive power. Why don't we find a rule that puts together the following elements: {*the, banana, be, diagonalize*} (or those in (56))? The formalism (notation) allows it. Further, the evaluation metric claims this grouping is exactly as "cheap" as Chomsky's "v," which is also an abbreviation for four completely distinct symbols. We would expect many languages to have rules treating elements like "v," M, *have,* and *be* alike, but surely no language has a rule remotely like the Negation Transformation that does something to *the, banana, be,* and *diagonalize,* and not to anything else. That's totally unexplained as long as Boolean *or* is allowed into the formalism for grammar.

We have to solve this problem somehow. It's obvious what direction the solution should take, but saying that isn't the same as actually giving a solution. The direction of the solution is to say that *there are no Boolean statements in SAs*—in particular, for this instance, that items that seem to be related by *or* are actually of the same category (Ross's approach).

At this point let me briefly mention Boolean *and*. In work done in the 1960s, transformations were occasionally written with something that appeared to be Boolean *and*, where, for example, a portion of the structure is something *and* is something else. One instance was an *extraposition* process that moved a clause rightward out of an NP to the end of the sentence. The SA was written something like this:

(149) X – [$_{NP}$ NP – S] – Y

An example is shown in (150).

(150) I saw [a man   ] yesterday [who had long hair]

In (149) the portion of the structure between X and Y is simultaneously NP and NP followed by S. Stated as a Boolean condition, this might look like (151).

(151) X – NP – Y
       and
       X – NP – S – Y

But here we run into a difficulty reminiscent of the one we ran into with Boolean negation. (151) actually imposes a much weaker requirement than (149) intended, since (151) doesn't guarantee that the very same portion of the structure that is an NP is also an NP followed by an S. Instead, it merely guarantees that somewhere in the structure there is an NP and somewhere in the structure there is an NP followed by an S. Like Boolean negation, Boolean *and* turns out to be pretty useless in the description of human language.

Chomsky's conceptual argument against quantificational conditions is right: they allow too wide a range of grammars. Boolean conditions allow a vast set of grammars too, though perhaps not as vast as the set allowed by quantificational statements. If we can show that Boolean conditions aren't needed either, we will really help solve the explanatory problem of how a child faced with limited data homes in on the right grammar. The fewer possibilities there are, the easier the task is. But saying this and making it work are very different things. Let's see, then, whether Boolean conditions really are needed in the theory.

2.6.2.2 Away with Boolean Conditions?

Recall that for the moment we have the following SA for the Word Boundary Transformation T21a:

(152) *T21a Word Boundary Transformation*
      SA (revised): X – Y (where X ≠ Z "v" or Y ≠ "Af" W)[20]

We've fixed up Chomsky's rule in two ways. First, the rule now states not just that the first portion shouldn't *be* a "v" (which was too easy to satisfy), but that it shouldn't *end* in "v." Similarly, the second portion shouldn't begin with "Af." Second, we're imposing on "≠" in both statements an explicitly quantificational interpretation. We're saying that to know whether this rule applies, it's not enough to find one element of the PM that satisfies the negative statement. We have to check all the (relevant) elements of the PM, and they *all* have to satisfy the requirement. That's a universal quantificational condition. As intended, it allows us to generate *John slept* but not **John sleep did*. But it runs afoul of Chomsky's learnability problem.

Our ultimate desire is to get rid of all this machinery: explicit quantification, implicit quantification, and even Boolean statements. In some cases substantial revision will be needed. To get rid of *or*, we will follow Ross and say that all the elements in "v" behave alike because they're all of the same category. For Chomsky there were four different categories. Similarly, we will say that all the elements under "Af" are of the same category. For Chomsky there were at least three different categories. The notion of *natural class* is obviously relevant for such phenomena. (Phonology had realized this long before syntax. *Or* can't be used in writing rules in phonology. Any time phonologists want to use *or* in writing a rule, it's because they don't realize the targeted items are a natural class of items, sharing a distinctive feature.) Now, saying that the items under "v" are of the same category and making it work are two different things. Chomsky actually had pretty good technical reasons for not putting these things together. Let's look at some of his reasons. First, notice what would happen with a rule like this:

(153) V → be

Is there a sentence or derivation where it might make a difference whether *be* is a V or not? Consider the most likely candidate for such an analysis, a sentence lacking any other verblike element.[21]

(154) John is a hero

Let's look at the hypothesized PM in (155).

(155)

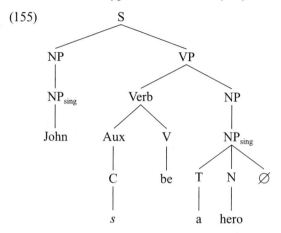

We've modified the PS rules to begin to address Ross's concern: the reason *be* behaves like a verb is that it *is* a verb.[22] Is there any reason why Chomsky didn't say that *be* in (155) is a V?

A technical reason is this. Suppose we were trying to apply Subject-Aux Inversion T18 to the PM in (155). Can we find an element of this PM that satisfies the SA of Subject-Aux Inversion? Yes, the element in (156) satisfies the SA (74a).

(156)   NP C V NP

(74)   a. NP – C – V X

So, we can apply Subject-Aux Inversion, ending up with the PM in (157).

(157)

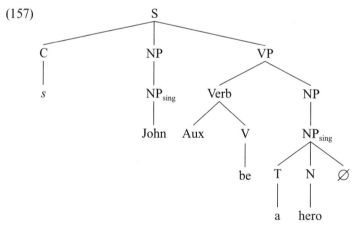

Can Affix Hopping T20 apply now? No, since *s* is no longer adjacent to *be*. Can the Word Boundary Transformation apply? Yes, and when it does, it puts a word boundary before *s*, setting the stage for *Do*-Support T21b. We will thus incorrectly generate **Does John be a hero?* The grammar has overgenerated. Has it also undergenerated?

Starting from (155), is there any way we can also generate *Is John a hero?* under current assumptions? Look at (155) again. We can find a string satisfying NP – C + be – X, which is one of the SAs for Subject-Aux Inversion, namely, (74d). One such string is *NP C be NP*. We can therefore apply the transformation and the new PM will be as shown in (158).

(158)

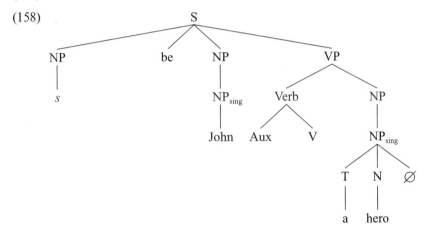

To this new PM we can apply Affix Hopping, so we can correctly generate *Is John a hero?* The result of our change was therefore *overgeneration*, but *not undergeneration*. We can still generate the old good sentences, but we also generate some new bad ones.

Another way to represent this state of affairs is to compare Chomsky's structure in (159a) (slightly corrected from his VP → *be* predicate; see *Syntactic Structures*, p. 67) with our hypothesized structure in (159b).

(159) a.   b.

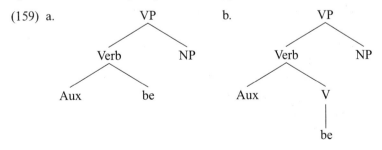

This is a rare case where one PM is a subset of the other. Every element of the PM in (159a) is an element of the PM in (159b). In other words, (159b) doesn't take away any possibilities that existed in (159a). All the elements of the PM in (159a) are still there; our modification just adds some new ones. Any element of the PM the grammar might have had use for before is still available, but now some new ones are available as well. Anything the grammar could do before, it can still do, but now it can do some new things as well. Therefore, it doesn't undergenerate—but it does overgenerate. That's the primary reason why Chomsky said that *be* isn't a V.

Unlike *be*, Chomsky argued, *have* in English sometimes (i.e., as a main verb) *does* allow two analyses, one as simply itself, the other as V. That's why the following questions are both possible:

(160) a. Have you any money?
      b. Do you have any money?

Note that this ambiguity of analysis isn't available for *auxiliary* verb *have*.

(161) a.   Has John left?
      b. *Does John have left?

Thus, main verb *have* is introduced under V, allowing it to be analyzed two different ways. Auxiliary *have* is of no category at all, allowing it to be analyzed just one way: as *have*.

Eventually, we will arrive at an analysis like Ross's that eliminates the need for the disjunctions in Chomsky's rules.

2.7   LEARNABILITY AND LANGUAGE ACQUISITION

2.7.1   Quantitative Problems

This theory makes available a vast number of grammars compatible with any set of data the child might hear. How does every child learning, say, the same dialect of English stumble on the same grammar? Here are some of the difficulties. Suppose that there are N transformations in the grammar and suppose that the child has figured out all those N transformations. Imagine that now all the child has to figure out is whether each rule is optional or obligatory. In that case the child has to consider 2^N grammars. Each of the N rules has two possibilities (optional or obligatory), and, by hypothesis, these possibilities are independent of those for any other rule; hence, $2 \times 2 \times 2 \times \cdots = 2^N$. As N gets big, as it indeed does in this theory, 2^N gets exponentially bigger.

Rule ordering poses a similar quantitative problem. Suppose again that the grammar has N transformations. Then they can be ordered $N!$ possible ways.[23] The first rule is any one of the N rules, the second is any one of the remaining $(N - 1)$ rules, and so on. Of course, as N gets bigger, $N!$ gets huge.

2.7.2   Qualitative Problems

In addition to the quantitative problems we just saw (too many grammars), we should consider possible "qualitative" problems. Do children have access to the kinds of data they need to figure out what the grammar is?

2.7.2.1   Optional versus Obligatory Rules

Optional rules are unproblematic in this regard. We observe (or the child observes) that English speakers can say *John hit the men* or *The men were hit by John*. Since both these sentences exist, we know (and the child knows) that the Passive Transformation T12 is optional.

The evidence that we use (or the child uses) to figure out that the Passive Transformation is optional is *positive evidence*. By contrast, to determine that a rule is obligatory, we, as linguists, use *negative evidence*, the information that certain sentences are unacceptable. For example, Affix Hopping T20 is obligatory; consequently, any sentence where it could have applied but didn't is bad. As scientists, we know how to gather that information. But how does the child? Children apparently don't have negative evidence available; they aren't systematically corrected for producing ungrammatical sentences in any useful way. Further, children don't even make the kinds of mistakes that might indicate that they make incorrect choices with respect to Affix Hopping. If children aren't even making mistakes of the sort we're interested in, then it doesn't make sense to ask whether they're corrected or not.

This problem is "qualitative" in that the necessary *type* of data isn't available to the learner. We will eventually end up with a modified theory of verbal morphology that will try to retain the descriptive power of this theory but that will be more explanatorily adequate (more on negative evidence below).

2.7.2.2   Rule Ordering

In addition to obvious quantitative learnability problems, rule ordering poses potential qualitative problems. Here is an artificial example illustrating the point. Suppose we have a phrase structure grammar that produces structures with the symbols J, K, and L, in that order. Now suppose the grammar has two optional transformations, as follows:

(162) *Transformation 1*
      SA: J – K – L
      SC: $X_1 - X_2 - X_3 \rightarrow X_1 - X_3 - X_2$ (Permute K and L when K is immediately preceded by J)

(163) *Transformation 2*
      SA: J – L – K
      SC: $X_1 - X_2 - X_3 \rightarrow r + X_1 - X_3 - X_2$ (Left-adjoin r to J when J is immediately followed by L)

With the strict ordering T2 > T1, we can produce the sequences JLK and JKL, depending on whether we elect to apply T1 or not. These are the only possibilities; T2 will never be applicable. With the reverse strict ordering, T1 > T2, we can again produce JKL (by doing nothing) and JLK (by applying just T1). But we can also produce rJLK, by applying T1 first, then T2. A child who is trying to learn the first of these languages but mistakenly guesses the second will be in the strictly overgenerating situation we saw with optional rules vis-à-vis obligatory ones. So here too, if negative evidence isn't systematically available, the child could have a dilemma.

2.7.2.3   Variable Placement

There is yet another technical device in *Syntactic Structures* that suffers the same explanatory problems. Imagine a transformation whose SA has three constant terms A, B, and C, in that order. Suppose for simplicity that each one of them is a single terminal or a single nonterminal. The theory presented in *Syntactic Structures* makes available a rather large number of SAs all of which satisfy the following criteria: they have three constant terms A, B, and C, in exactly that order. How many SAs will fit the schema ABC? The answer is $2^4 = 16$, since there are four positions where a variable might or might not occur. The situation is illustrated in (164), where X, Y, Z, and W are variables.

(164) X A B C   X A Y B C   A X B Y C   X A B Y C Z
       A X B C   X A B Y C   A X B C Y   A X B Y C Z
       A B X C   X A B C Y   X A Y B Z C   X A Y B Z C
       A B C X   A B X C Y   X A Y B C Z   X A Y B Z C W
                                                          A B C

How does the child figure out how many variables are in an SA and where those variables are? There's clearly a quantitative problem here. Now we'll see that there's also a qualitative problem.

Suppose the child thinks that the SA for the rule is *A B C X* whereas in reality it's *A B C*, and suppose the rule is optional. We then have the situation in (165) (still regarding a language as a set of sentences).

(165)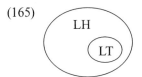

    LH: Hypothesized language (with the SA *A B C X*)
    LT: Target language (with the SA *A B C*)

LH is a superset of LT. Everything that is a sentence of LT is also a sentence of LH, but not conversely. Whenever a PM satisfies *A B C*, it automatically satisfies *A B C X* as well (since any string, including the null string, satisfies a variable). But a PM might satisfy *A B C X* without also satisfying *A B C*. Thus, the transformation can apply in more cases in LH than in LT. What kind of problem does this raise? If a child guesses LH, we as linguists can tell that the child is wrong, because he or she will be producing ungrammatical sentences. But the child, in order to figure out that he or she is wrong, would have to be so informed. As mentioned before, however, we assume, with most other researchers, that children don't receive negative data. More significantly, empirical studies on language acquisition have shown that children make surprisingly few syntactic mistakes when learning language. How is it possible that children don't make mistakes? Proposals have been made about this, and they're sort of on the right track, but we'll see that fundamentally they miss a point. One proposal is the *Subset Principle*, as named by Berwick (1985). (The principle was actually proposed earlier by Dell (1981), who called it *grammars in the inclusion relation*.) Berwick offers two potential interpretations for the Subset Principle. The interpretation that's relevant here is this: Whenever a child is confronted with a choice between two grammars that generate languages such that one is a proper subset of the other, the child will compute this relation and will first guess the grammar that gives the smaller language, the subset language. Then, if the child is wrong, there will always be positive evidence to indicate the error.

Two things seem wrong with this proposal, though. One is that the computation we're forcing the child to do is tricky in general, namely, to compare two grammars with respect to whether one generates a subset language of the other. In more recent work it has become clear that what this proposal is based on seems to be the most dubious part of the whole theory, namely, that a language is, in fact, a set of sentences. It seems pretty coherent to say that a language is a set of "machines" cranking things out in the brain, but to say that a language is a set of sentences isn't obviously coherent. It's a claim that raises many questions. For example: What set of sentences? Where are they? How do we know what the set of sentences is? But all of this is what the child has to rely on to do this computation, which is one reason to be skeptical of the Subset Principle as a learning heuristic.

Here's another reason to be skeptical: Notice what the Subset Principle says in this particular case, and in fact in general. It says something exactly counter to what's always been claimed in research into phonology. Mainstream research in generative phonology, going back virtually to its origins in the 1950s, says that the simpler and more general a rule is, the more likely it is that the child will guess that it's the right rule. But the Subset Principle says exactly the opposite, that the least general rule in the whole set is what the child will guess first.

An alternative way of solving the "subset problem" is to avoid it altogether. Suppose the problem never can arise: the language faculty is organized in such a way that the child is never confronted with a choice between languages such that one is a proper subset of another. Research from the last couple of decades makes this look more and more plausible. As we go on, we'll look at theories of language that have, or at least approach, this property.

2.7.3   More on Negative Data

I think too much of a fuss has been made about negative data. Notice that it isn't true, as many people seem to assume, that if we find out that children really do encounter negative data, our whole field will come crashing down. The quantitative problems would still exist. Given a mid '50s style theory, there are too many grammars available. How are children going to sift through 50 billion grammars, even if they have negative data? Further, there are other sorts of qualitative problems, such as the lack of very complicated sentences in the data. Finally, as McCawley (1992) has observed, the standard anecdotes illustrating the lack of effect of negative evidence when it *does* occur (in the form of explicit corrections) would seem to demonstrate lack of effect of *positive* data as well, since the corrections in the standardly cited scenario take the form of an instruction to use a correct form provided by the corrector.

On the standard assumptions about negative data, which we will continue to adopt here (though without great confidence), overgeneration is a big problem. Undergeneration, on the other hand, is never much of a problem. That's the usual situation we expect children to be in. Before learning each new word, the child is in a situation of undergeneration. Children escape undergeneration by hearing new "positive" data.

2.7.4 Summary

Recapitulating the discussion in this section, it appears that any theory with the following features fails to attain explanatory adequacy:

- Optional vs. obligatory rules
- Extrinsic ordering in rules
- Complicated structural analyses (SA can have any number of terms, allowing the grammar to include a vast number of transformations.)
- Complicated structural changes (SC can consist of any number of elementary operations, also allowing for a vast number of transformations.)

Ideally, an explanatory theory shouldn't have any of these devices. If so, then we have to figure out whether eliminating them results in overgeneration, and we have to see whether there's any way of limiting this overgeneration without reinstating the acquisition problem. Descriptively, the *Syntactic Structures* rules (as we've fixed them) work pretty well, but in terms of explanation, the question remains: how is it that the child, faced with limited data, arrives at the correct grammar rather than any one of 72 billion other possibilities?

2.7.5 Optional/Obligatory Rules Revisited

In light of the previous discussion, let's look again at the problem of learning whether a particular rule is optional or obligatory. There are four possible situations, the first two of which we can easily dispense with (here I'm assuming, for ease of exposition, that everything is held constant except that one particular rule is optional or obligatory).

(166) | | *Hypothesis* | *Target* |
|---|---|---|
| Situation 1 | Obligatory | Obligatory |
| Situation 2 | Optional | Optional |
| Situation 3 | Optional | Obligatory |
| Situation 4 | Obligatory | Optional |

There are in principle three ways that a hypothesis and a target can mismatch: overgeneration, undergeneration, or both. Situation 3 produces only overgeneration. Anything that can be generated with an obligatory rule can also be generated with the optional version of that same rule. However, if the rule is optional, additional sentences can be generated. On the other hand, situation 4 produces only undergeneration. A child who hypothesizes that a particular rule is obligatory will apply it to every structure that fits it. But if the rule is actually optional in the target language, then all the sentences the child's grammar produces are grammatical in that language, as well as all the sentences that result from not applying the rule.

▪ *Yamane:*   What is a situation where we would get both overgeneration and undergeneration?

Lasnik: That hasn't arisen in the cases we've been discussing. But it can happen if the child, for example, guesses the wrong ordering of rules. Recall that it also happened with the Word Boundary Transformation T21a and *Do*-Support T21b, where mistakes were cropping up: unacceptable sentences with *Do*-Support in place of (rather than in addition to) acceptable sentences without *Do*-Support.   ▪

There are two technically simple ways to avoid the optional versus obligatory dilemma. Since the dilemma only arises if the child has to figure out whether a given rule is optional or obligatory, it disappears if *either* all rules are obligatory *or* all rules are optional. Since at this point the former possibility seems to result in such drastic undergeneration, I will pursue the latter. In that case the grammar will clearly overgenerate: every derivation available with obligatory rules is also available with optional versions of those rules, but not conversely. The task will then be to find a way to limit this overgeneration, but in such a way that any devices we introduce don't themselves recreate the same quantitative and qualitative learnability problems. I will turn to this task very shortly.

2.7.6   Rule Ordering Revisited

Given two transformational rules, TM and TK, Chomsky considered only two possibilities: either TM is ordered before TK (TM > TK) or TK is ordered before TM (TK > TM). This is a *total* ordering. If the right ordering is TM > TK and the child hypothesizes TK > TM, both undergeneration and overgeneration might result. The wrong order could lead to the generation of a bad sentence and could, at the same time, prevent the generation of a good one.

However, there's another possibility, which Chomsky didn't discuss in *Syntactic Structures*: namely, *partial* ordering. That is, in a given list of rules there might be pairs of rules between which no ordering is specified. Imagine that in the child's hypothesized language TK > TM, whereas in the target TK and TM are freely ordered. Imagine further that TK and TM are optional. In this case the child's grammar will undergenerate. Derivations with TK > TM should be allowed but won't be. On the other hand, suppose now that the right grammar has strict ordering and the child hypothesizes a free ordering. In that case the child's grammar will overgenerate, as this is just the reverse of the previous situation.

Overgeneration is always a problem if we assume that there is no negative evidence, because the only way to correct overgeneration is by somehow being informed that one's grammar is overgenerating—that is, by being informed that some of one's sentences are ungrammatical. So, if the very widespread (but not necessarily valid) assumption that there is no negative evidence is correct, we want to make sure that the situations leading to overgeneration never arise.

Suppose some rules are strictly ordered and some rules are freely ordered. That is true, as a matter of fact. Some of the orderings in *Syntactic Structures* are stipulated for no empirical reason. So, it's perfectly fine to say that some rules are freely ordered while others are strictly ordered. But this could cause trouble for children. The Subset Principle might help them out of it. But now we would have to say that given the whole grammar, particular orderings are always more highly valued somehow than free orderings. But which particular orderings? And what kind of evaluation metric does that entail? No evaluation metric of the type we've been talking about will give this result. And it shouldn't. We would like the more general grammar to be the most highly valued. And free ordering is much more general than strict ordering. In principle, then, this criterion suggests a solution: all rules are *freely ordered*. This way the child only has to learn the rules, and doesn't have to learn how to order them.

2.7.2 Variable Placement Revisited

Suppose that we have an SA with the constant terms *A B C*. Now suppose that there aren't 16 SAs available as in (164); there's only one, namely, the most general one: *X A Y B Z C W*. As with obligatory rules and rule ordering, assuming the most general case is a desirable move on explanatory grounds. But if we hypothesize that there are always variables between constant terms, so that it never matters whether two terms are next (adjacent) to each other, or whether one term is adjacent to one end or the other of the sentence, the results are usually correct, but some descriptive problems arise, in particular with the rule of Affix Hopping T20. Let's look again at Chomsky's SA for Affix Hopping.

(167) X – "Af" – "v" – Y

Now consider what happens when we insert a variable between "Af" and "v."

(168) X – "Af" – Z – "v" – Y

(168) will lead to overgeneration, because Affix Hopping will be able to occur even if something intervenes between the affix and the verb—for example, negation, leading to results like *John n't left*. Affix Hopping turns out to be about the only case where adjacency is actually required in the SA of a rule, suggesting that we're missing something about this process. I will return to this point directly.

For Chomsky, an SA like *A B C* meant, "Find an element of the PM that begins with an A, immediately followed by a B, immediately followed by a C, immediately followed by nothing." Under the assumption that adjacency isn't relevant in SAs, I will impose a different interpretation on *A B C*: "Find an element of the PM that anywhere in it has an A and anywhere later has a B and anywhere later has a C." That is, if variables are always assumed, they never need to be explicit. This interpretation is conceptually better because it captures the phonologists' insight that a more general rule takes fewer symbols to write.

We're assuming that the more general the rule, the cheaper it will be. Having variables in the SA of our rules will make them more general. So, if all rules indeed have variables, as almost all do, and in all positions, then we're home free—our rules will indeed be cheap. But if there turn out to be some renegade rules that need to stipulate adjacency (perhaps Affix Hopping), those will be costly. Then we might posit a new symbol, an "adjacency symbol"—the opposite of a variable symbol.

Chomsky was led into positing a "nonadjacency symbol." We are led into positing an adjacency symbol. This is just an empirical question. Is it more likely for a syntactic rule to specify adjacency or not to specify adjacency? Is it more normal for syntactic rules to care whether elements are adjacent to each other, or not to care? It seems much more normal for them not to care. Under the evaluation metric of the '50s and '60s, we can make rules that don't care about adjacency cheaper—more highly valued

—by saying that there's no symbol that we have to put in rules to say that elements aren't necessarily adjacent, but there is a symbol that we have to put in to say that elements are adjacent.[24]

2.7.8 The Stranded Affix Filter and the Architecture of the Grammar

Let's see how a theory with only optional rules, no ordering, and no stipulated adjacency works. In terms of explanation, it's great. In terms of description, it works about two-thirds well. I've claimed that most of the adjacency that's stipulated in *Syntactic Structures* is gratuitous (a quick inspection of Chomsky's rules shows that it does no real work), so there's no need to stipulate it. Half of the rules are optional, so if our theory assumes only optional rules, it accounts properly for those. Much of the ordering is stipulated, perhaps because of Chomsky's desire to make the list a total ordering. So, all we have to account for is the residue: a few rules labeled obligatory, and a few true orderings (i.e., cases where applying rules in the wrong order results in an ungrammatical sentence).

Now notice the following startling fact. The rules in *Syntactic Structures* are involved in a huge conspiracy: the large majority of the explanatorily problematic devices in *Syntactic Structures* are there to ensure that all affixes are attached. Plausibly, that's why Affix Hopping and *Do*-Support are obligatory. In other words, the rules describe but don't capture the following overwhelming generalization:

(169) A stranded affix is no good.

So, we might instead say that all rules are optional, all rules are freely ordered, and "A stranded affix is no good." Why bother stating (169) in terms of intricate rule ordering? Why bother stating obligatoriness as a "footnote" on six rules? Why not factor it out?

This solves the quantitative problem extremely well. But there's still no solution for the qualitative problem. Doesn't (169) demand negative evidence? How can we solve the qualitative portion of the acquisition problem for this theory? To do this, we must say that (169), which we can call the *Stranded Affix Filter*, doesn't have to be acquired; it's part of (inborn, wired-in) Universal Grammar. The theory in *Syntactic Structures* makes the claim that there could be another language just like English but where Affix Hopping is optional. The theory we're looking at now (pretty much that found in Lasnik 1981, developing research described in Lasnik and Kupin 1977 and Chomsky and Lasnik 1977) makes the claim that there couldn't be any such language. To the extent that there isn't such a language, the theory that says that Affix Hopping is obligatory is discon-firmed, and the theory proposed in Lasnik 1981 is confirmed. So, with (169) we not only gain in the description of English—to the extent that it's true, we gain in the description of all languages as well.

Under these assumptions, the grammar might look as shown in (170).

(170)   Phrase structure rules

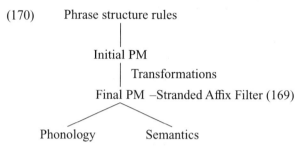

Under this model, transformations are optional, they are unordered, and they do not stipulate adjacency. They also do not have Boolean or quan-tificational conditions. Every term is a single terminal or nonterminal (to capture structure dependence). It will also be desirable to limit how many terms an SA can have (maybe three—or perhaps two or even one).

This model of the grammar addresses many of the problems we've been discussing, but not all of them.

Exercises

1. The two questions in this exercise concern negative evidence.

A. Discuss some specific property of a rule or a grammar that would require negative evidence (i.e., the information that a particular example is ill formed) in order to be learned. Be as explicit as possible, and show precisely why negative evidence is needed in the case you discuss.

B. Show how the property you discuss in question A could be eliminated in favor of a device (or devices) not requiring negative evidence. Again, be explicit.

2. Suppose that we modified Chomsky's Negation Transformation T16 so that it could freely insert either *not* or *n't*. Show how we could then derive some gram-matical sentences with *not*. Do any problems arise? Discuss.

3. Suppose we discovered a language that was like English except that the fol-lowing ungrammatical sentences were grammatical:

*Does Susan be winning?
*John swims not

Discuss how the *Syntactic Structures* account would have to be changed to ac-commodate such a language. Make the smallest possible change. What additional consequences would your change have?

Chapter 3

Verbal Morphology: *Syntactic Structures* and Beyond

3.1 PROBLEMS IN *SYNTACTIC STRUCTURES*

In the previous chapter we considered several important theoretical issues arising from Chomsky's analyses in *Syntactic Structures*. One of these issues presents a potential problem for the theory, namely, the fact that the evaluation metric and the notational device don't discriminate as to what group of elements can be a term in a rule; any group of elements can constitute a term, even if they don't form a natural class (Ross's problem; see section 2.5.1). We've discussed a possible approach to solving this problem. Now let's identify some other problems with the *Syntactic Structures* theory and discuss how Chomsky and others have tried to handle these problems.

3.1.1 (In)transitive Verbs

One seemingly trivial problem is the following. Recall that *Syntactic Structures* has a PS rule for generating transitive verbs:

(1) VP → Verb NP

But there's no rule for generating intransitive verbs like *sleep*. Perhaps such a rule would look like this:

(2) VP → Verb

Would having both (1) and (2) in the grammar create a problem? The answer seems to be yes. Consider the following sentences:

(3) a. John slept
    b. John solved the problem

The problem is that nothing seems to prevent the grammar from generating structures like (4a) and (4b).

(4) a. 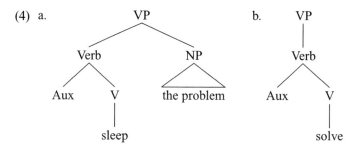   b.

With the two rules (1) and (2) the grammar can generate *John solved the problem* and *John slept* but also **John slept the problem* and **John solved*. If we say that all verbs are transitive, by including only rule (1) in the grammar, then this problem doesn't arise. But then we don't know how to generate *John slept*.

So, how can we introduce intransitive verbs into the system without overgenerating? In *LSLT* Chomsky proposed that there are two verbal categories: V_t (takes an object) and V_i (doesn't take an object). Even within the category V_t, verbs differ: we can say *John solved the problem* but not *John solved the hot dog*. Chomsky therefore proposed that there are many kinds of V_t: for example, some that take *problem* as an object, and others that take *hot dog* as an object. So there are V_{t_1}, V_{t_2}, V_{t_3}, and so on. Significantly, all these Vs behave exactly alike except with respect to whether they take an object, and the kind of object they take. Isn't it suspicious that all the V_ts behave exactly like the V_is except in whether they take an object? Apparently, we're missing a huge generalization.

In *Syntactic Structures* there was no revealing way of handling the (in)transitive verb problem. However, in *Aspects* Chomsky solved this problem (see section 2.4) with the machinery of *subcategorization* (meaning that there's a "big" category of verbs with smaller "subcategories," each with their own properties) and *selection*. We'll consider this new machinery (and some of its subsequent development) in detail shortly.

3.1.2   The Problem of *n't* and *not*

The (in)transitive verb problem and Ross's problem are the more or less technical/conceptual problems we want to solve. There are also a few empirical problems we need to look at, described here and in sections 3.1.3–3.1.5. In *Syntactic Structures* Chomsky proposed a rule determining the distribution of *n't*, but no rule determining the distribution of *not*. We want to figure out the distribution of *not*, which is tantalizingly similar to the distribution of *n't*, but not identical.

(5) a. John can swim
    b. John can't swim
    c. John cannot swim

(6) a. John swims
    b. John doesn't swim
    c. John does not swim

(7) a. Doesn't John swim?
    b. *Does not John swim?

(8) a. Does John not swim?
    b. *Does John n't swim?

If *n't* and *not* were totally independent, there would be no problem; we would just say that they're introduced by different rules. But they're so similar that we need to account for the fact that they're not identical in distribution.

3.1.3   *Do*-Support

Here's the descriptive generalization regarding *Do*-Support T21b: it's a last resort. It applies only if there's no other way of keeping an affix from being stranded. In *Syntactic Structures* Chomsky captured the fact that *Do*-Support is a last resort operation by making it obligatory and ordering it after certain other transformations, the last of which is Affix Hopping T20. If Affix Hopping can't apply, then we're left with *Do*-Support. But now recall, in light of the discussion in section 2.7, that we don't want the grammar to include any obligatory rules, or any rule ordering. We need some other way of capturing the essence of this descriptive generalization.

3.1.4   Structure Dependence

In *Syntactic Structures* Chomsky formulated transformations that affect nonconstituents, such as Subject-Aux Inversion T18. Obviously, however, there's a basic intuition, one of the guiding insights of the whole theory, that transformations are structure dependent, that they only affect constituents. Chomsky was already relying on this intuition in the '50s, as evidenced by his arguments in *Syntactic Structures* that the effect a transformation has on a sentence reveals its constituent structure. If transformations are structure dependent, that reasoning is sound. If transformations aren't structure dependent, then what transformations do to a sentence doesn't say anything about its structure—it only tells what things happen to be next to other things. Since we surely do want to capture structure dependence, we have to eliminate some of these problematic rules and find something to replace them with.

3.1.5   A Call for the "X-Bar Theory"

Another issue that came up in *Syntactic Structures* is that the theory developed there allowed PS rules like (9) but none like (10).

(9)   NP → ... N ...

(10) NP → ... V ...

Why is this? The formalism allows both rules, and the evaluation metric judges them equally costly.

In what follows we'll begin to address some of the problems outlined above. Let's start with the last one.

3.2   X-BAR THEORY

Chomsky didn't come to grips with the question of why rules like (10) don't exist until the late '60s in "Remarks on Nominalization" (published in 1970 but written and circulated a couple of years earlier). There he proposed that there are no individual PS rules of the sort that did so much work in *Syntactic Structures* and even in *Aspects*. Rather, there's what came to be called the *X-bar schema*. X is a variable, ranging over category names such as V, N, and so on.

Here's the version of the X-bar schema that Chomsky presented in "Remarks on Nominalization":

(11) X′ → ... X ...
     X″ → ... X′ ...

(12) X″
     |
     X′
     |
     X

N′ and N″ are true complex symbols. Remember that in *Syntactic Structures* NP looked like it had something to do with N, but in that system it really didn't. NP was just one symbol that was written for mnemonic purposes with two letters. In the X-bar theory, a category label is a letter plus a number of bars (originally written as overbars—e.g., $\overline{X}$—but later written as primes—e.g., X'—for typographical convenience). It can be thought of as an ordered pair. X is $\langle X, 0 \rangle$, X' is $\langle X, 1 \rangle$, and X'' is $\langle X, 2 \rangle$. The idea is that we start with a lexical category X (e.g., N or V) and "project" upward to an intermediate projection X', which always has to include the X by definition (it might also include other elements); then X' projects further up to X'', which has to include the X', which in turn includes the X (and might include other elements as well). The X-bar theory thus immediately explains why there are no rules like (10). Another way to describe this is to say that phrases have *heads*, or that phrases are projections of heads. A head has as its sister a *complement* (or complements). For example, in the following rule, NP is a complement of V:

(13) V' → V NP

There's a major difference between English-type languages, where the complement always follows the head, and Japanese-type languages, where the complement always precedes the head. English and Japanese are particularly pure instances of this. In English the complements follow the verb in VPs (*hit the ball*), NPs (*destruction of the city*), and PPs (*on the table*). In Japanese VPs, NPs, and PPs, the order is the opposite. So, there's good reason for thinking that all these configurations are parts of the same phenomenon.

Eventually, we'll explore a stronger version of the X-bar theory, a biconditional version that Chomsky didn't present in "Remarks on Nominalization": namely, phrases have heads, and heads project. Whenever a structure has an XP, it has an X (this is what Chomsky proposed in "Remarks on Nominalization"), and whenever a structure has an X, it has an XP.

3.3 SUBCATEGORIZATION AND SELECTION

3.3.1 The Base Component

Recall that in *Syntactic Structures* the base component is the component of the grammar that gets the derivation started. It consists only of the context-free PS rules (those listed on page 111 of *Syntactic Structures*). In *Aspects* Chomsky developed a new version of the base component, proposing that it has three parts:

1. A context-free PS grammar whose terminal symbols are prelexical categories (i.e., not *swim* or *John*, but V or N)

2. A lexicon (which lists all the words and their idiosyncratic properties)
3. Lexical insertion transformations, which take items from the lexicon and insert them in the structures created by the PS grammar. Why are they transformations? For the same reason that the Number Transformation T15 in *Syntactic Structures* is a transformation: because they're context sensitive as a result of subcategorization and selection (e.g., they can insert *solve* only if the PS grammar has generated a structure with a direct object, and they can insert *swim* only if it has generated one with no direct object).

There are two major differences between the theory of the base proposed in *LSLT* and *Syntactic Structures* and the theory proposed in *Aspects*. One is that whereas there's no distinction between lexicon and transformational component in *Syntactic Structures*, in *Aspects* the lexicon is factored out of the transformational component. Another is that in *Syntactic Structures* there's no recursion in the base component. The PS rules generate "little" structures, and to get bigger structures we apply generalized transformations that merge these little structures. For example, the *LSLT* theory derives *John knew that Mary left* from the separate structures underlying *John knew it* and *Mary left*. A generalized transformation (GT) embeds the second in the first. In *Aspects* Chomsky advanced a major argument that this procedure is incorrect. The argument is based on the fact that one kind of derivation permitted by GTs never seems to be needed, namely, the kind where a singulary transformation (i.e., one operating on a single PM) must apply in the "matrix" before another clause is inserted in it by a GT.

In *Aspects*, instead, the base is recursive, and there are no GTs. The unneeded derivations are excluded by the principle that transformations apply cyclically. The *principle of cyclicity* says, "Begin a transformational derivation on the deepest clause and work steadily up the tree." Recursion in the base gives rise to one of the seemingly most significant innovations of *Aspects*. There is now a new level of representation, *D(eep)-Structure*, which arises after all PS rules and all lexical insertion transformations have applied, and before any other transformations apply. The level of representation that results from applying all the transformations is *S(urface)-Structure*.

3.3.2 The Lexicon

There is (or should be) an intimate connection between PS and the lexicon. The lexicon expresses everything idiosyncratic a speaker knows about lexical items. To take an example, when we know the verb *solve*, we know

- Its phonological representation
- Its syntactic category: V
- That it takes a direct object (and that the direct object must denote something that is problemlike). The subcategorization frame of *solve* then is SOLVE [____ NP].
- That it has an NP subject (and that it presumably must be some "higher animate")
- Its meaning

(If it were an irregular verb like *bring*, some of its inflected forms (e.g., *brought*) would be specified in the lexicon as well.)

Let's look at how the lexicon works in further detail. The X-bar theory makes available numerous head-complement relations like these:[1]

(14) a. V′ → V NP
      b. V′ → V PP
      c. V′ → V S

Consider the lexical entries for some verbs:

(15) a. see [____ NP]
      b. talk [____ PP]
      c. think [____ S]

Chomsky made the point in *Aspects* (a point that obscures a much deeper point) that the existence of a PS rule like (14a) implies the existence of a lexical entry like (15a), because if there were no lexical entry like (15a), then the PS rule (14a) would never have a chance to operate. How would speakers even know that their language had this rule? If there were no verb of English that took a direct object, what would be our evidence that there is a PS rule that says a verb can take a direct object? Similarly for (14b) and (14c), and for (15b) and (15c). The converse is also the case.

This means that for at least this portion of the PS system in (14), the head-complement portion, there is total redundancy. Chomsky pointed this out in *Aspects*, but didn't say that it's a problem. Presumably, though, we have to get rid of either (14) or (15). The rules in (14) say that there can be a verb that takes a direct object, a verb that takes a prepositional phrase, a verb that takes a clausal complement. (15) states exactly which verbs can do those things. When we know English, we don't just know that there's some verb that takes some particular element, we know exactly which verb. Thus, if we have to choose between getting rid of (14) and getting rid of (15), we have to choose getting rid of (14), because we have to have the information in (15), the idiosyncratic information about lexical items. In a sense, this seems bizarre, because the entire theory of PS that Chomsky developed in *LSLT* was based on PS rules and PS derivations, which generated initial PMs. PS derivations are impossible without PS rules; yet this argument indicates that PS rules don't exist. Very interestingly, Lasnik and Kupin (1977) actually proposed what seems to be a theory of PS that doesn't have any place for PS rules.[2] A bit later Stowell (1981) proposed that PS rules are redundant with other principles and idiosyncratic lexical properties (see section 1.2.6.2). Once we set the "head parameter" (distinguishing Japanese from English, for instance),[3] once we talk about individual properties of lexical items, once we add one more module, Case, then the PS rules are rendered superfluous.

So, how do we formalize PS? One possibility is to adopt Lasnik and Kupin's approach. We say that any set of strings is a PM, as long as it satisfies certain well-formedness conditions: those given by the X-bar theory, those related to consistency (two elements of the PM can't be saying contradictory things about the order of the words, or about dominance relations), and those following from completeness (nothing in the terminal string can be left out of the constituent structure representation). So, a set of strings needs to satisfy consistency, completeness, and the X-bar theory (regarded as a well-formedness filter). If it does, then it's a PM; otherwise, it isn't.

Further considering redundancy and the lexicon, it has always been known that there's a close connection between selectional restrictions and meaning. Obviously, *solve* can take *problem* as its object and not *hot dog*, and *eat* can take *hot dog* as its object and not *problem*, precisely because those verbs mean what they mean. It's simply unimaginable that the next language we look at would have words that mean the same thing as *solve* and *eat* but have the reverse selectional restrictions. This connection is so tight that we would hope that the selectional restrictions could reduce to the meaning—though, presumably, not conversely, since there are verbs that have identical selectional restrictions but still don't mean the same thing (e.g., *deny* and *assert*). Carrying this reductionist program further, let's assume that since selectional restrictions and meaning are redundant, we'll get rid of selectional restrictions and keep meaning. The slight problem with this is that we have a way of formalizing selectional restrictions (e.g., the one in *Aspects*) but we have no clear idea of how to formalize lexical meaning; we just know it's there. We'll have to leave this task to the semanticists.

When we know a word, we know its meaning and its selectional restrictions, but we've decided (although we haven't worked out the theory yet) that if we know the meaning, we don't have to know anything in addition to tell us the selectional restrictions.

What about subcategorization? Intuitively, in the mid and late '60s linguists had in mind that selectional restrictions might be semantic, but they regarded subcategorization as straightforwardly syntactic.[4] However, Pesetsky (1982) argued that if we know the meaning of a word, we know its selectional restrictions *and* we know virtually everything about its subcategorization. For example, if we know the meaning of *eat*, we know it will occur in a frame like this: [____ NP]. If we know the meaning of *believe*, we know it will occur in frames like these: [____ S] and [____ NP]. Pesetsky's point was that subcategorization is predictable from meaning also. He more or less combined meaning and selectional restrictions and called the conglomerate *semantic selection* (s-selection). The way he put it was that semantic selection *entails* subcategorization, or, in other terms, *categorial selection* (c-selection).

■ *Vukić:* Wouldn't a suggestion like that run into problems with words that mean exactly the same thing but take different complements?

Lasnik: Interestingly, pretty much the first day this was proposed I raised that question, but a few years later I decided my objection might not be correct. Logically, it was correct, but I was making an empirical assumption that that kind of situation turns up all the time. And then I decided that at least the cases that I brought up at first, I was misanalyzing. This is discussed to some extent in Chomsky and Lasnik 1993. For example, the verb *eat* can take a direct object or not. How can we possibly predict that? We can say both *I ate* and *I ate lunch yesterday*.

Vukić: As compared with *devour*, which has to take a direct object.

Lasnik: Yes, so we have a real problem. We have two verbs with very similar meanings but different subcategorization frames, and we have one verb that seems to have two different subcategorization frames. We have to look at a lot more data. But cases like these have an interesting semantic property. There's nothing semantically wrong with sentence (16), where *eat* takes an NP, even though it's pragmatically odd.

(16) When I walked in, John was eating his shoe

Now compare *eat* without an NP, as in (17).

(17) When I walked in, John was eating

(17) can't mean that John was eating his shoe—it can only mean that he was eating a meal. Virtually all the classic English examples of verbs with "optional" direct objects are like that. There are no semantic constraints on what the object can be if it's there, but if there isn't any object, all of a sudden, there *are* semantic constraints on the interpretation: the missing object is understood as prototypical or else specialized. (*Drink* and *smoke* are two more examples parallel to *eat*.) This suggests that we're dealing with two different verbs *eat*, with different semantics, hence different subcategorization. Is it crazy to think that there are two different verbs *eat*, one transitive, one intransitive? I don't think so, because, as a matter of fact, the intransitive one has a synonym, *dine*.   ■

A full Pesetskyan program would lead to adopting a proposal that is very popular in the acquisition literature, called *semantic bootstrapping*, according to which if we learn the meaning of a word, we don't need to learn anything more about its syntax.[5]

3.3.3 Theta-Roles

In *Aspects* Chomsky observed that although selection goes both "left" and "right," subcategorization only goes one way. That is to say, verbs select both different kinds of objects and different kinds of subjects (some take an animate subject, some take an inanimate subject, etc.). However, although some verbs need an object and some verbs won't tolerate an object, all verbs need a subject—there's no subcategorization with respect to subjects. In *Lectures on Government and Binding* (1981) (henceforth *LGB*) Chomsky gave the requirement that all clauses have subjects a special name: the *Extended Projection Principle* (EPP). (The Projection Principle itself characterized this connection between aspects of meaning and subcategorization.)

Pesetsky (1982), following work by Chomsky, who in turn was following work by Gruber in the late 1960s (see Gruber 1976), related all this to *thematic roles* (now often called *theta-roles*). Backing up a bit, let me mention arguments and predicates. Roughly speaking, *arguments* name individuals in the universe of discourse; *predicates* name properties in the universe of discourse. For example, consider (18).

(18) John asserted that Mary was intelligent

Here *John* and *that Mary was intelligent* are arguments of the predicate *assert*. Now consider (19).

(19) John hit Bill

Here *John* has the theta-role of *agent* (roughly, the intentional causer); *Bill* has the theta-role of *patient* (roughly, the thing affected). In (18) *John* is again agent and the complement clause has the theta-role *theme*. The idea is that (1) there is a limited set of theta-roles for arguments (some of which are agent, patient, theme, goal, and instrument), and that (2) predicates have associated with them sets of theta-roles, what Stowell (1981) called *theta-grids* (e.g., *hit* in (19) has an agent theta-role that has to be connected to the subject and a patient theta-role that has to be connected to the object).

In *LGB* Chomsky proposed a condition on the association between arguments and theta-roles, the *Theta-Criterion*, a special case of the Projection Principle.

(20) *The Theta-Criterion*
    a. All theta-roles must be assigned to arguments.
    b. Every argument must have a theta-role.

Let's look at some examples.

(21) *Mary devoured

The verb *devour* has a patient theta-role that it has to assign, but there's nothing there to receive that theta-role. So (21) violates the Theta-Criterion, in particular case (20a). Here's another example:

(22) *Mary slept Bill

The verb *sleep* has only one theta-role to assign, an *experiencer* theta-role, which in (22) is assigned to *Mary*. The NP *Bill* is an argument that ends up with no theta-role. Therefore, (22) violates the Theta-Criterion, in particular case (20b).

This eliminates the problem that led Chomsky to deal only with transitive verbs in *Syntactic Structures*. He dealt only with transitive verbs because dealing with intransitive verbs as well would have required two categories, and this would have led to a huge version of Ross's problem. Remember our earlier question: why do V_ts (transitive verbs) and V_is (intransitive verbs) behave alike in every way except that one is inserted in a VP like (23a) and the other in a VP like (23b)?

(23) a.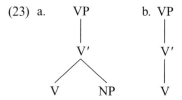

We can eliminate that problem by saying that the lexical entry of a verb includes information about what kind of V' it can be inserted in. This is idiosyncratic information. The behaviors that all verbs share aren't idiosyncratic; they simply constitute what it means to be a verb. The behaviors that are peculiar to individual verbs have to be specified in the lexicon; these have to be learned. Children don't have to learn how verbs in general behave, but they do have to learn how *solve* behaves. This is the crucial claim that's being made.

There's a fair amount of redundancy hidden in this particular concept of lexical entry, and we'll see a way to get rid of it. To say that the object of *solve* has to be "problemlike" is to say that *solve* has an object. But the subcategorization frame of *solve* also says that it has an object. The obvious solution, Pesetsky's, is to eliminate subcategorization.

3.4   ENGLISH VERBAL MORPHOLOGY REVISITED

3.4.1   Inflection as a Syntactic Entity

Now we're going to reanalyze English verbal morphology in light of the X-bar theory and our new views of subcategorization/selection. Let's start by looking at (24).

(24) John left

What happens if we propose the structure in (25) for sentences like (24)?

(25)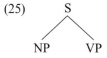

(25) doesn't conform to the X-bar schema we've been talking about. The X-bar theory says that phrases have a head, and (25) doesn't have a head. S isn't a projection of anything. Interestingly, at the time that Chomsky was introducing X-bar theory, he ignored this problem. In "Remarks on Nominalization" he said that everything except for sentences conformed to X-bar theory. Sentences were generated with a special non-X-bar rule.

(26) S → NP VP

In allowing this difference, Chomsky seemed to be missing a generalization. Then, in the mid '80s, he did fit S into the X-bar theory (see *Barriers* (Chomsky 1986)). What could the head of S possibly be? The head of S is what Chomsky called *C* in *Syntactic Structures* and *Inflection* in work of the mid '80s and beyond (so as not to confuse it with C of Complementizer; see below). In other words, Chomsky proposed that the head of a sentence is the inflectional element that merges with the verb.

Let's think about this proposal for a moment. We're forced to say that *something* is the head of S if we want a full-blown version of the X-bar theory (call it the *extended X-bar theory*), and there are really only two reasonable candidates, which are discussed again and again in the literature. One candidate is the inflectional element. Even though this element looks as if it's merged with the verb, we have all the evidence from *Syntactic Structures* that it starts out as an independent item. The other candidate is V. However, the idea that V is the head of the sentence will be hard for us to support if we want to maintain the converse of "Phrases have heads," namely, "Heads project." We know from *Syntactic Structures* that it seems irreducible that the inflectional element is an autonomous syntactic entity. So, even if we decide that S is a projection of V, the inflectional element will have to project also. What could it possibly project to, if not S?

By that line of reasoning, let's assume that sentences are actually a projection of the category Inflection (Infl or I, for short), and see what the structure of the sentence *John left* might be.

(27) John left

(28)

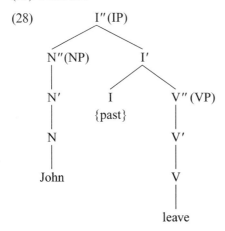

In (28) VP is the *complement* of I, and NP is the *specifier* of I. Specifiers and complements are those phrases that occupy the positions marked in (29).

(29) a. X″ → (specifier) X′

   b. X′ → X (complement)

      or: X′ → (complement) X (as in Japanese, for example)

In one respect (29) looks radically different from the system in *Syntactic Structures*: we've taken the inflectional element out of the VP (though even Chomsky probably had that in mind). But in another respect (29) isn't that different: we've still captured the insight that the inflectional element is an autonomous syntactic entity.

■ *Depiante:* What's the structure of sentences with modals?

Lasnik: Chomsky actually is more explicit about *have* and *be* than about M (modals). As I read Chomsky's more recent work, he claims that M is just I. There's another possibility, of course, if we want to fully capture Ross's generalization: that a modal is a kind of verb. Of course, under the extended X-bar theory, it has to project, so if we say a modal is just a modal, then it has to project some kind of modal phrase; if it's a verb, then it has to project some sort of verb phrase. Let's take the latter approach, following Ross. Recall that Chomsky did have a minor argument for this point of view (see section 1.3.2). If M were an "alternative" to tense, then modals would be untensed, but Chomsky argued that modals are tensed (the "sequence of tenses" argument).

(30) a. John says he can swim

   b. John said he could swim

(31) a. John says he is happy

   b. John said he was happy

It looks like the sentences in (30) display the same phenomenon as the ones in (31). If tense is the key to this phenomenon, and if M is an alternative to tense, then we don't have a way of describing that fact. In conformity with these assumptions, we have structure (33) for (32).

(32) John must leave

(33) a

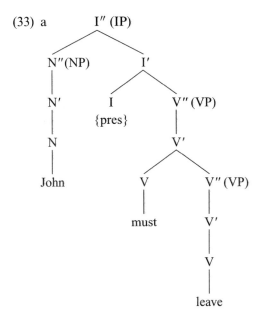

What's special about a modal under this view is that it's a verb that takes a VP as its complement. A modal isn't an instance of I, but it's just like I in that it takes VP as its complement. That's a rare property that modals and I share, unexplained at this point.   ■

Now, what's the structure of sentences containing other auxiliaries, such as *be* in (34)?

(34) John is singing

There are two things we want to do: we want to incorporate S into X-bar theory, and we want to solve the selectional problem that Chomsky solved just by saying that *be* and *ing* are introduced as sisters and are of no category at all. (35) shows an initial attempt.

(35)

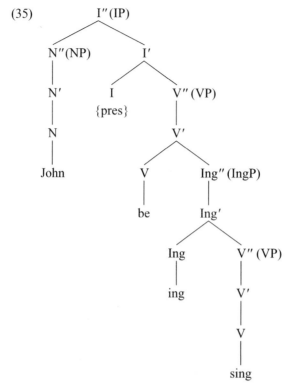

Ing is a minimal element, hence a head, which therefore projects a maximal projection. We can call it an *Ing Phrase* (IngP) or a *Progressive Phrase*. Now, what about the very close connection between *be* and *ing*? We aren't able to capture it quite the way Chomsky did. The closest connection available in the *Aspects*-style theory is the complement relation, so we make the IngP the complement of *be*. This is close enough that we can establish whatever selectional restrictions we need. It's then just a selectional property of *be* that the complement it takes can be an IngP.

If we continue to assume something like Affix Hopping T20, as we will, then the {pres} morpheme could merge with *be* by Affix Hopping, giving *is*. The *ing* will merge with *sing* to give *singing*. We are thus claiming that the relationship between *ing* and *sing* is analogous to the relationship between {pres} and *be*, which is just what Chomsky said in slightly different terms in *Syntactic Structures*.

Notice that we need a way of "stacking up" auxiliaries. Consider (36) and its structure in (37).

(36) John must be singing

(37)

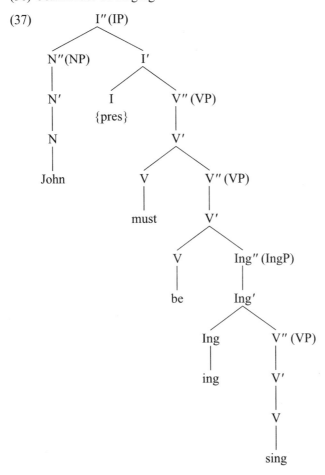

We treat *have* and *en* just like *be* and *ing*. *Have* heads a VP and its complement is an *En Phrase* (EnP). In this way we capture the dependency between *have* and *en* and between *be* and *ing*: *have* selects an EnP and *be* selects an IngP.

Now consider how Subject-Aux Inversion T18 might work within the X-bar theory, particularly with respect to the troublesome *Do*-Support T21b examples.

(38) a. John left
      b. Did John leave?

Chomsky's basic approach is still available. We could just say that somehow {past} moves to the front of IP. However, in a more restrictive
theory of grammar, we not only want to restrict the theory of phrase
structure, which we've done, we also want to restrict the theory of transformations. We want to restrict the class of structural analyses (which
we've discussed a lot), but we also want to restrict the class of structural
changes. In particular, it isn't obvious that permutation is indeed an option. Either permutation isn't an option, or it's literally like blowing on a
mobile, taking two things that are sisters and switching their order. That
was always our concern about permutation in *Syntactic Structures*, where
two elements that weren't sisters were permuted. For those reasons we're
strongly tempted to try to find an alternative way of doing Subject-Aux
Inversion. What could that alternative be? To answer that, a brief digres-
sion is in order. There are certain kinds of words that introduce sentences:
that, *whether*, and so on. Rosenbaum (1967) called them *complementizers*,
words that make sentences into complements. How do we fit a complementizer into the structure for a sentence such as (39)?

(39) I think *that* John is crazy

The extended X-bar theory tells us how we have to fit it in. *That* isn't a
maximal projection, so it must project to a maximal projection. If we
adopt Rosenbaum's name for it, *complementizer* (C), then C projects a
Complementizer Phrase (a CP), with IP as the complement of C.

(40)

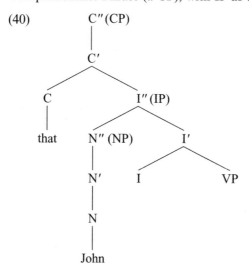

Sometimes the C is *that*, as in *I think that John is crazy*. But consider (41).

(41) a. I think John is crazy

   b. John is crazy

One might imagine there's a C in (41a) but that it's silent. Is there any other place where we need a head that's silent? One case is the present tense (non–3rd person singular) null morpheme. So, there's at least the possibility that a complementizer could also be silent, or that C could even be empty, for that matter. Let's try that. Suppose we have a structure like (42).

(42)

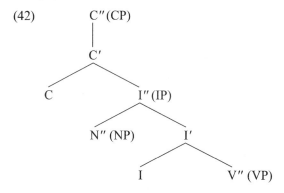

Now we have a way to do Subject-Aux Inversion without permutation: I moves to C. It turns out that once we start looking at things like this, we find that many transformations in the world's languages work the same way: one head moves to the next head position up, a process that has come to be called *head movement*.

3.4.2   The Structure of Complementizer Phrases

Let's discuss the CP/IP structure a bit further. There's a relation between the specifier of IP and the head I. That relation has traditionally been called subject-verb agreement but it's really subject-I agreement. (Chomsky proposed a rule much like that in *Syntactic Structures*, namely, Number Agreement T15: C (i.e., what we're now calling I) takes whatever form it takes depending on the features of the subject.) Now we can define the relation even more precisely as specifier of IP–head of IP agreement. The past decade of research has revealed overwhelming evidence that specifier-head agreement is extremely common in the languages of the world.

Once we establish this relation, we have a handle (not really a solution yet) on one of the residual problems in *Syntactic Structures*: the stipulated dependency between T_w T19, the rule creating and fronting interrogative expressions like *who* (*wh*-phrases) (usually called *Wh*-Movement), and Subject-Aux Inversion. In terms of the CP hypothesis, how do we describe what happens when *Wh*-Movement applies? What happens is that the *wh*-phrase moves to the specifier position of CP. Although Chomsky didn't say this in "Remarks on Nominalization," in his later work on X-bar theory, in *Barriers*, he proposed that complements and specifiers are always maximal projections. Notice that the *wh*-phrase is surely a maximal projection. If we take this seriously, that specifiers are always maximal projections, and if we notice that *Wh*-Movement always moves something that's a maximal projection, we can combine these two observations by saying that *Wh*-Movement moves a *wh*-phrase to the specifier of CP. But then one more thing has to happen, namely, Subject-Aux Inversion, since (44) is an acceptable English sentence but (43) isn't.

(43)   *What John will buy?

(44)   What will John buy?

The necessity of Subject-Aux Inversion here has occasionally been analyzed as another sort of specifier-head agreement. In particular, the *wh*-phrase in the specifier of CP has to agree with C, and this agreement demands that something occupy C. It's an instance of what Kuroda (1988) called *forced agreement*. We haven't proven that this analysis is right, we haven't even spelled it out in much detail, but if we want to pursue it, it really demands that I move to C. If I is merely adjoined to IP, the structure has no special properties since adjunction has no special properties. Adjunction positions are merely created to order, whereas specifiers and heads are there by virtue of the way the structure is defined.[6]

It appears to be true also that in all languages that have this kind of "I-raising," it operates in the direction of the complementizer. So, in English-type languages it always seems to work leftward. In Japanese-type languages it always seems to work rightward. Again, it isn't obvious why that should be so if I-raising is merely adjunction to IP, but it follows immediately if I-raising is movement to the head.

3.4.3 Movement to a Specifier Position

Let's see how our theory is shaping up. It has the following elements:

1. X-bar theory
2. The notion of IP
3. The notion that modals, *have*, and *be* are verbs
4. The notion that Subject-Aux Inversion is an instance of I-to-C movement
5. *Wh*-Movement (moving a *wh*-phrase to the specifier of CP)

Are there any other rules that move an element to a specifier position? Part of the Passive Transformation T12 does something a lot like that. Look at the following sentence:

(45) John was arrested by the police

John is the understood object of *arrest*, not the subject. All of its selectional restrictions show that it's the object. Thus, the thing that can appear as the subject in a passive sentence like (45) is something that has to satisfy what would have been the object's selectional restrictions in the active. We don't want to repeat those selectional restrictions for every passive sentence in the language; hence, we want to say that *John* started out as the object in (45) (the very argument that Chomsky made in the 1950s). Where does *John* move to? We know it moves to the front of the sentence, but what position in the structure does it move to? Not any old position at the front of the sentence, but the specifier of IP. How are we so sure that's where it is? Because it agrees with the I as shown in (45), repeated here, and in (46).

(45) John *was* arrested by the police

(46) John and Bill *were* arrested by the police

So, we should add point 6 to our list above:

6. Specifier-head agreement

Ideally, we would like to limit transformations pretty much to the two effects we've just seen:

(47) a. XPs moving to specifier positions
     b. X^0s (heads) moving to head positions

That will be our goal.

3.4.4   The Head Movement Constraint

Returning to the details of Subject-Aux Inversion, recall that in the *Syntactic Structures* version T18, C (now I) and the first auxiliary verb (if there is one) move to the front of the sentence. At the moment, our theory doesn't seem to allow anything to move except I by itself, so in fact it can generate (48),

(48) Did John leave?

but it can't generate (49),

(49) Can John leave?

and it might incorrectly generate (50).

(50) *Does John can leave?

This problem is a variant of the one we saw earlier, namely, how to formally state that *Do*-Support T21b is a last resort.

To address this problem, let's start with (49), which presumably has the underlying structure in (51), assuming that modals are Vs.

(51)

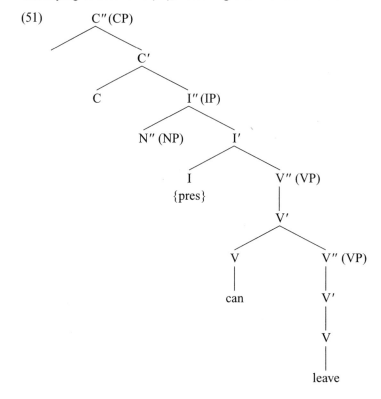

To get the modal *can* to move to C, we first raise *can* and adjoin it to I, and we then raise the whole I complex to C.[7] We end up with the tree in (52).[8]

(52)

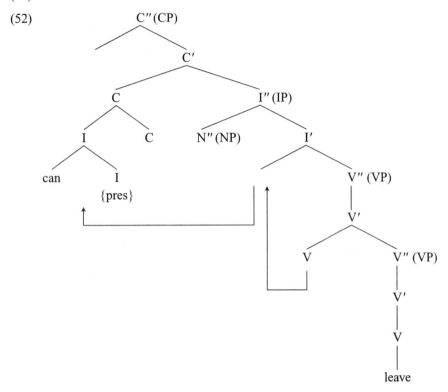

Note that (as with the negative sentences in *Syntactic Structures*) apparently the rule of I-to-C movement must obey some version of the A-over-A Constraint. It's the higher I, not the lower one, that has to move.

Now we have a way of deriving *Can John leave?* Let's call this *successive head movement*. V raises to I, a process attested in many languages, and then I raises to C, another common process.

What if we skipped the "V-to-I raising" step and directly raised the V (in this case *can*) all the way up to C? In that case we would get the questions in (53).

(53) a. *Can John {pres} leave?
    b. *Can John does leave? (if *Do*-Support applies)
    c. *Can John leaves? (if Affix Hopping applies)

Evidently, the only way to move *can* is to move it successively, first to I, and then to C. Movement can't just skip the I position. This kind of phenomenon, in several instantiations, was discovered by Travis (1984). She called it the *Head Movement Constraint* (HMC), which says that if a head moves, it can only move to the very next head up. Another example, of a sort Chomsky discussed in *Barriers*, is (54).

(54) *Be John will happy?
      (cf. Will John be happy?)

Example (54) is possibly more convincing than (49) since (54) relies on the existence of bare *be* and finite *will*, whereas (49) assumes bare *can*, which doesn't obviously exist.

There are various versions of the HMC. Furthermore, movement to specifier position is subject to a similar constraint; if something is going to move to specifier position, it's going to move to the next specifier position up. It can't skip a specifier. Rizzi (1990) generalized these two constraints as *Relativized Minimality*: If an item is going to move, it's going to move to the next appropriate position up. Rizzi's constraint is called *Minimality* because an item moves in a "minimal" way to the next appropriate position up, and *Relativized* because where the item lands depends on what it is. Roughly speaking, if it's a head, it moves to the next head position up; if it's an XP, it moves to the next XP position up. An XP can cross over a head, but not over a specifier. A head can cross over a specifier, but not over a head. Travis's HMC thus becomes a special case of Rizzi's Relativized Minimality (RM).

So, (54) violates the HMC, an instance of RM, because *be* has moved directly all the way to C, skipping a couple of head positions. On the other hand, (55) obeys the HMC. *Will* is the higher verb in the structure, so it moves to the next higher head, which is I, and from there it's carried by I to the next higher head, which is C.

(55) Will John be happy?

There are a few remaining problems. Why doesn't English have (56) instead of (57)?

(56) *Left John?

(57)   Did John leave?

We don't want to be "too hard" on (56) because there are many languages that allow questions of exactly this form. We want to say that there's some rather superficial property of English that doesn't allow this. What is the property? In *Syntactic Structures* Chomsky merely stipulated a list of items that move to the front of the sentence with I. We'll also need some sort of stipulation, but it can't consist merely of a list of items that move with I, because we believe so strongly in structure dependence. Rather, what we have to stipulate is a list of items that are or aren't allowed to raise to I. So, what will we say? We will say that modals, *have*, and *be* indeed *are* allowed to raise to I, but other verbs of English *are not* allowed to raise to I. In this way we can rule out (56) (of course, our list embodies Boolean *or*, a problem we'll have to return to).

3.4.5   Negation

Now let's see how negative placement would work within the X-bar theory. Suppose that negation is structurally located between IP and VP. Irrelevant details aside, the extended X-bar theory would suggest a structure like (58).

(58)

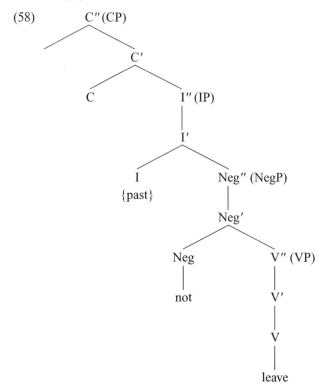

Then the ungrammaticality of (59) immediately follows from the HMC.

(59) *John left not

In particular, (59) could come about only if *leave* raised to I over *not*, which doesn't happen in English. However, in languages such as French, verbs can raise to I, and sentences like (59) are possible. Even in English, raising is possible with a modal, *have*, or *be*.

(60) a. John will not leave
     b. John has not left
     c. John is not here

The structures that Chomsky accounted for in *Syntactic Structures* by the identical SAs in the Negation Transformation T16 and Subject-Aux Inversion T18, we're accounting for by head movement, namely, verb raising to I, plus one stipulation, namely, that modals, *have*, and *be* are the only verbs that are allowed to raise in English. Of course, that limitation is still unexplained.

Here's the problem we have to solve to make this work (and we're now at the frontiers of current research). We've just said that *not* is somewhere in the tree in (58). The extended X-bar theory says that if *not* is there, it must be either a head or a maximal projection. It isn't a maximal projection, or at least it doesn't seem to be, so it must be a head. That's why (59), repeated here, violates the HMC.

(59) *John left not

But then, when the modal, *have*, and *be* move in (60), they also violate the HMC.

Example (61) conceivably satisfies the HMC. We can say that *can* amalgamates with negation and then the whole complex amalgamates with I.

(61) John can't leave

But what about (62), where *can* and negation haven't amalgamated?

(62) John can not leave

We might say that *can* and *not* are indeed amalgamated here, but the reduction hasn't yet taken place. But then what about the cases in (63)?

(63) a. Can John not leave?
     b. Will John not leave?

The examples in (63) are crucial. They look like flagrant violations of the HMC. There are about a dozen really fancy ways in the literature to keep these sentences from violating the HMC. To the best of my knowledge, not one of them really works. We'll be looking at a couple of these proposals (including Chomsky's recent work).

As long as we can say that *not* is just hanging around somewhere, we can account for negation. But as soon as we adopt the extended X-bar theory, indicating that *not* is a head, then movement across negation will violate the HMC. Interestingly enough, in some of his recent analyses for the main verb cases, Chomsky explicitly says that they violate the HMC, but he has to do a lot of fancy footwork to keep verb movement in French and auxiliary verb movement in English from violating it as well. We will explore more modern statements of the HMC to see how Chomsky tries to distinguish main verbs from auxiliary verbs in this context.

3.4.6 Affixal I and the Nature of the Head Movement Constraint

Consider the structure (65) underlying (64), assuming, for ease of exposition, that modals are instantiations of I, or have already raised to I (irrelevant details aside).

(64) John must be happy

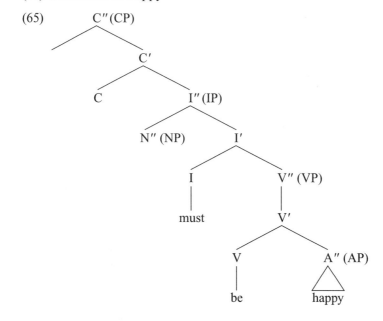

If we move *be* to C, we get the following question:

(66) *Be John must happy?

This is the classic illustration of the HMC, the one given above, and the only one Chomsky gave when he first took up these matters in *Barriers*. It involves moving a head (*be*) across another head (*must*), as shown in (67).

(67)

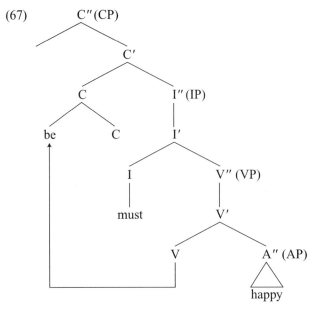

To be honest, though this argument is standard, I've never entirely accepted it. The reason is that although there's overwhelming evidence in English for a process that raises I to C, there's no evidence whatsoever for a process that raises V to C. If there's no process that raises V to C, the issue isn't that we've violated the HMC by doing this, the issue is that we've tried to apply a rule that English doesn't even have.

Yet suppose that, regardless of this, we accept the argument that the HMC is preventing the movement in (67). Then there ought to be another way to construct a derivation. We should be able to move *be* and adjoin it to *must* in I, and then move the whole complex to C, ending up with (68) or (69).

(68) *Must be John happy?

(69) *Be must John happy?

If we continue to assume something like the A-over-A Constraint, once we've moved *be* up and adjoined it to I, we won't be able to move *be* itself further, but we should be able to move the whole complex further.

Clearly, we have to block this derivation. Here's a plausible descriptive generalization: V can raise to I only if the I is an affix; V can't raise to I if the I is a freestanding lexical item. A similar generalization can be made for Affix Hopping. Affix Hopping appears to be head movement, but instead of head raising, it appears to be head *lowering*. Now, we know that affixal I can lower to V, but there's no evidence that a modal can ever undergo Affix Hopping.

What's going on? We seem to be looking at two instances of the same constraint. The only time head movement can ever take place from I to V is when the I is an affix. This suggests a concept that has formed the basis for a huge amount of work in the last 10 years. We only do operations if there's a "reason" to do them. There's a reason for raising V to an affixal I, because the affix needs something to hang on to; but there would be no reason for raising V to a lexical I. Similarly, there might be some reason for lowering an affixal I to a V, again because the affix needs something to hang on to, but there would be no formal reason for lowering a lexical I to V. The way this generalization is often stated is, "Movement is a last resort." That's very tricky, because we've already concluded that *Do*-Support is a last resort. Which one is really the last resort? We need to see what happens when they're in competition. If Chomsky was right in *Syntactic Structures*, it looks like when they're in competition, movement isn't the last resort. Movement happens if it can, and *Do*-Support happens if movement can't. We can still say that they're both relative last resorts. Either movement or *Do*-Support happens if it has to, if there's an affix that would otherwise be stranded. Under this analysis, syntactic processes are, in effect, driven by morphological requirements, an idea at the heart of many recent approaches to syntax, especially the "minimalist" approach.

Let's now reconsider and see what happens if we accept the *Syntactic Structures* assumption that even when a sentence has a modal, it also has an inflectional morpheme. The relevant structure is shown in (70).

(70)

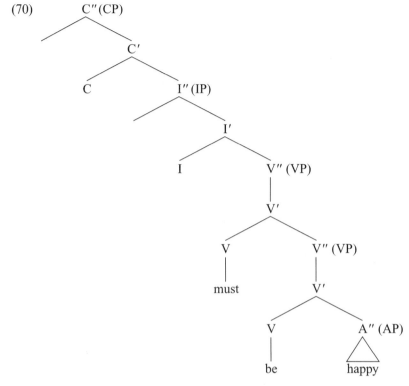

Now, finally, we might be in a position to construct a more convincing argument for the HMC. Why can't English speakers say (71) and (72)?

(71) *John is must happy

(72) *Is John must happy?

Obviously, in (71) and (72) *be* has raised to I across an intervening head, *must*.

But even here there's an equivocation: where do bare forms occur in English? There are a number of places where they occur. One is after modals. But modals don't occur after modals. Another is after *to*. But modals don't occur after *to*, either. Where do modals occur? They don't occur in the bare form (e.g., *to can*), the perfect form (*canen*), or the progressive form (*caning*). They only occur in the present form (*can*) and the past form (*could*). How do we say that? I'm not sure how to do better on that point than classical grammarians do when they're taking about verbs with similar properties in Latin. They list them, and they call them "defective" verbs—defective in that they occur in certain forms and not in others. That seems to be exactly the case with modals. They're like verbs in that they seem to exhibit tense morphology, but they're unlike all other verbs in the language in other respects, not occurring in any of these other forms. We have to say that somehow. In the theory we're talking about, we know where to say it: in the lexicon. If this behavior is listed in the lexicon as an idiosyncratic property of these verbs, then the above derivation that violates the HMC, (70), is also trying to construct something that morphologically doesn't exist in English. If it's *be* that associates with the *s* in I, then *must* won't have any tense morpheme to associate with; hence, it will be bare. But *must* just doesn't occur bare in English.

It's really rather amazing how hard it is to find evidence in this realm for the HMC. The constraint is almost universally accepted by transformationalists, on the basis of examples like these. The interesting thing is that in all the examples there seems to be something else going on. The HMC thus seems redundant, at least for these phenomena.

At this point let's restate our theoretical assumptions for English verbal morphology:

- V-raising to I (nonmain verbs)
- I-raising to C
- I-lowering to V (main verbs)

V-raising to I, which is a very common process in European languages (and even in earlier English), is restricted in Modern English. Only modals, *have*, and *be* can raise to I. That's why in English it looks like Affix Hopping has to exist. We have to get the affix together with the verb, but when the verb is a main verb, it can't raise. Let's look at how we could go about explaining that, and how a child could possibly learn it. Because surely it would be more general and simpler to assume that all verbs raise.

One way the child might know that main verbs don't raise is this. We've said that *Do*-Support and movement are last resort operations. Suppose that movement is the "next to the last resort" and that *Do*-Support is truly the last resort. Hearing a sentence like *Did Susan see the man?* and knowing that *Do*-Support is a last resort operation, the child might conclude that the simpler, more general way (raising the verb) is unavailable.

■ *Depiante:* Could we say that all verbs raise to I in English and that there's no A-over-A Constraint? If we move the V to I and then the I to C, we can get *Did Susan see the man?*

Lasnik: I think that idea's worth pursuing, but I think we'll find two problems with it. One is that we'd need something stronger than the notion that there's no A-over-A Constraint. We'd also need to posit an "A-under-A Constraint." We'd have to *demand* that the lower element move. The reason is that if we merely say there's no A-over-A Constraint, then we get two ways of analyzing the structure, and we should get both results: *Did Susan see the man?* and *Saw Susan the man?* Further, if we want to go on assuming, as I think we almost have to, that *Do*-Support is a last resort, even if both results are available, the one with *do* shouldn't be possible if the one without *do* is possible.

The idea of adjoining one thing to another and then not moving the whole resulting complex as a unit, but just moving part of it (*excorporation*), is often assumed not to be possible. But a few linguists, starting with Roberts (1991), have argued that it is possible. For example, Watanabe (1993) proposes an analysis of verbal morphology that relies crucially on excorporation, and Bošković (1995) proposes an analysis of participle verb movement in Serbo-Croatian that also relies on excorporation. But for the purposes of our discussion, I'll continue to assume that excorporation doesn't exist.   ∎

To further explicate the HMC, I want to introduce something that right now will sound like mere notation, though very shortly we'll make use of it. Suppose we attempt a movement that violates the HMC, as in (73).

(73)

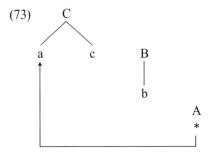

We can't move A to C, skipping B. How do we notate that this movement is wrong? Where do we put the "star"? It sounds at first like a pointless notational question, but we're going to see an analysis of Chomsky's that makes crucial use of a particular answer: the star goes in the position the item has moved from. (In this case we put a star on A.) Ross (1969b) provided some interesting evidence for this, which Chomsky didn't appeal to (though I admit that Ross didn't interpret his evidence quite the way I will here).

Ross proposed in his doctoral thesis (1967) that there's a whole family of constraints on movement, or, as he called them, *island constraints*. Later (1969b) he showed that the damage done when one of these locality conditions on movement is violated can largely be repaired by performing some kind of deletion operation. He cleverly showed a variety of constructions where something moves out of an island but where XP-deletion then takes place, deleting a big XP that includes the position from which the item moved. The deletion almost entirely repairs the sentence.

In our terms, we can say, following Chomsky, that violating one of these locality constraints puts a star in the position from which the item moved, but if a deletion operation follows, the star disappears.

Here's a way to make this more precise. In "Conditions on Transformations" (1973) Chomsky began to argue that when something moves, it doesn't just leave behind nothing; it leaves behind a silent instance of itself, often called a *trace*.[9] This view of the way movement works is called *trace theory*. So, in (73) the star is on the trace. In "Some Notes on Economy of Derivation and Representation" (1991) (hereafter "Economy") Chomsky argues that sometimes a trace created by violating the HMC can be deleted, in which case the sentence becomes acceptable.

Now consider French. Does French have I-lowering to V? Emonds (1978), followed by Pollock (1989), followed by Chomsky in "Economy," claimed that French doesn't have I-lowering to V. The intuition is that Affix Hopping is a kind of last resort. Raising V to I, if it can be done, is a better way of solving the stranded-affix problem than lowering the affix to V, and French does have V-raising to I.

Emonds and Pollock, followed by Chomsky, gave a couple of arguments for this point of view. One standard piece of evidence for this claimed difference between French and English is the following contrast:

(74) a.   John often kisses Mary
     b. *John kisses often Mary

(75) a. *Jean souvent embrasse Marie
     b.   Jean embrasse souvent Marie

In French the verb *must* raise to I, and that's why it appears to the left of the adverb (under the assumption that the position of I is higher than the position of the adverb). In English, we know independently that main verbs never raise to I. On the other hand, auxiliary verbs are able to raise, as seen in (76).

(76) John will often write books

In a restrictive theory of transformations what we would want to say about all of these cases is that they involve an operation we could call "Move Head." Now, we have overwhelming evidence that English and French both have "Move Head," so how do we account for the differences between them? In particular, how do we account for the fact that French has no I-lowering? "Move Head" seems to make both raising and lowering available.

I will sketch Chomsky's answer here, and later expand on it. The insight originally goes back to work by Fiengo (1977), who was instrumental in developing trace theory. Fiengo proposed something that he called the *Proper Binding Condition*, analogizing traces to anaphors, which are referentially incomplete expressions requiring "antecedents."

(77) a.   John injured himself
    b.   *Himself injured John
    c.   *Mary injured himself

The requirement on anaphors seems to be that the antecedent of the anaphor must come before the anaphor. On closer investigation, however, that requirement doesn't suffice.

(78) *John's mother injured himself

Why should (78) not be good? Notice that *John* precedes *himself* in the sentence. Reinhart (1976) argued that the antecedent of an anaphor has to be *higher* in the tree than the anaphor (in informal terms). That the subject is higher than the object accounts for the contrast between (77a) and (77b). But *John* in (78) isn't higher than *himself*, because it's inside another NP.

Fiengo analogized traces to anaphors to explain many of their properties. He thought precedence was relevant. He said that when something moves, it has to move leftward, because the antecedent of a trace has to precede the trace. But once we realize that the true requirement on anaphors isn't precedence but height, then we conclude that when something moves, it has to move "upward," because the antecedent of a trace has to be higher in the tree than the trace.[10]

Our conclusion entails that Affix Hopping, as an instance of lowering, isn't a desirable operation. This explains why languages don't like using it. So, we have to find out if there's any way to fix the violation. If there isn't any way to fix it, then we've explained the facts of French, and we've explained some of the facts of English (regarding auxiliary verbs), but we've ruled out *John left*. However, if we discover some way to fix the trace of the affix that lowered, then the sentence will be allowed.

3.4.7 Main versus Auxiliary Verbs in English

We don't yet have an account for the fact that auxiliary verbs and main verbs in English behave differently. Auxiliary verbs raise to I, but main verbs don't. In French, however, all verbs raise to I. Pollock (1989) is concerned precisely with these differences: the one between English and French and the one internal to English.

Following Pollock, we have to figure out (1) what the difference between main verbs and auxiliary verbs might be, and (2) what the difference is between French and English that would be relevant to the difference between main verbs and auxiliary verbs.

Pollock proposes that *main verbs have theta-roles to assign, but auxiliary verbs don't*. He also makes the following proposal:

(79) a. French I is morphologically rich.

      b. English I is morphologically poor.

(I'm simplifying slightly here, since Pollock argues that I is actually divided into Agr(eement) and Tense; see below.) Finally, Pollock makes the following suggestion:

(80) a. When I is morphologically rich, it is transparent to theta-role assignment.

      b. When I is morphologically poor, it is opaque to theta-role assignment.

In other words, if a V with some theta-roles to assign finds itself in the configuration shown in (81), it won't be able to assign those theta-roles.

(81)

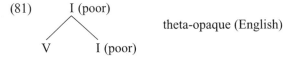

(Technically, V-raising means adjoining V to I as (81) shows.) The V can't "see out of" this I, which it's now inside of; that is, it can't "see" the arguments it's trying to assign the theta-roles to (this is, of course, still just a metaphor). On the other hand, if a V with theta-roles to assign finds itself in the configuration shown in (82), it will be able to assign those theta-roles.

(82)   I (rich)

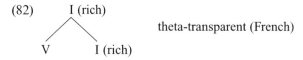

theta-transparent (French)

The V *can* "see out of" this I; that is, it can "see" the arguments it's trying to assign the theta-roles to.

Illustrating the same point with a concrete example, suppose we had a configuration like (83) in English, which is the (sub)structure we would get by V-raising.

(83)

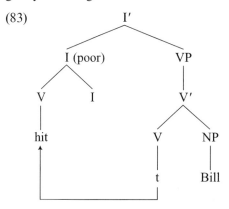

Since English I is poor, the I configuration in (83) is opaque to theta-role assignment. Therefore, *hit* won't be able to assign its theta-roles, and neither the subject nor the object will be able to receive a theta-role. (83) thus represents a triple violation of the Theta-Criterion.

■ *Gutiérrez:* How do we know that *hit* moves before assigning its theta-roles?

Lasnik: That's an excellent question. I never fully understood that aspect of Pollock's theory. In a theory of the *Aspects* sort, D-Structure is the level of representation relevant to theta-role assignment, so movement is irrelevant.

However, even in *Aspects* Chomsky acknowledged that some aspects of semantic interpretation don't seem to be deducible at D-Structure (e.g., scope of quantifiers). That led to the formulation of theories claiming that certain aspects of semantics are D-Structure phenomena and others are S-Structure phenomena. Such theories were pretty standard in the late '60s and early '70s. On the other hand, in the principles-and-parameters theory of *LGB*, D-Structure is irrelevant to semantic interpretation, all aspects of meaning ultimately being read off the surface.

That gives us a handle on Pollock's claim, but it still seems problematic. Much of the work that transformations do either destroys or drastically distorts what would have been theta-configurations. Trace theory provided a solution for that problem. When an NP moves, its trace receives the theta-role directly. The antecedent receives it indirectly via its association with the trace.

If all semantic interpretation is carried out at S-Structure, then movement must leave a trace. But if movement leaves a trace, and the trace has to have all the relevant properties of the thing that moved, then we still have the relevant configuration for theta-role assignment in (83).

Pollock must be assuming then that theta-role assignment isn't a property of D-Structure, and that either (1) when something moves, it doesn't leave a trace or (2) traces can't be used to determine theta-role assignment. Without these assumptions, Pollock's account isn't possible. But with these assumptions, standard examples of the *John was arrested* type become difficult, since the theta-role of *John* is the one connected with object position. In order to proceed, I put this problem aside.   ▪

Given Pollock's assumptions, why can auxiliary verbs raise in English? Because auxiliary verbs don't assign theta-roles, so raising them to an opaque I in English doesn't violate the Theta-Criterion. Of course, it isn't obvious that auxiliary verbs (especially modals) don't have a theta-role to assign, a point I will return to.

▪ *Vukić:* Where do Chomsky and Pollock assume that modals are generated?

Lasnik: As far as I know, neither Pollock nor Chomsky has looked in any detail at exactly where modals are in the structure. As a matter of fact, when Chomsky is pressed on this point, he often retreats to a position whereby modals don't cooccur with I and merge with it as in *Syntactic Structures*; rather, they occur as an alternative to the Inflectional morpheme that's generated in place of I. That's a logical possibility, and morphologically it isn't crazy. It's not nearly as obvious with modals that there's a tense ending as it is with main verbs, or even with *have* and *be*. The other possibility is to follow Ross's view that modals are verblike. If we say that, then we have the structure in (84).

(84)

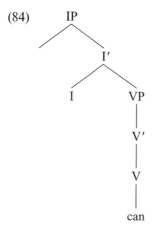

But if we say that modals have theta-roles, when *can* raises to I, it won't be able to assign its theta-roles since I is "poor" and theta-opaque. For this reason, Pollock assumes that modals don't have theta-roles while still admitting that they contribute to the meaning of the sentence.   ■

Pollock's account makes one strong prediction that I've argued is incorrect (see Lasnik 1981). It predicts that auxiliary verbs can always raise, in any kind of sentence, no matter how impoverished I is. However, we find that in imperative sentences in English, auxiliary verbs can't raise.

(85) a.   Do not be foolish!
     b.   *Be not foolish!

Auxiliary verbs also can't raise in infinitival sentences in English.

(86) a.   I believe John not to be foolish
     b.   I believe John to not be foolish
     c.   *I believe John to be not foolish

That isn't predicted by Pollock's theory.[11]

3.4.8 Summary

We've distinguished between the types of verbs that may undergo inversion with the subject: in French, all types of verbs; in English, only auxiliary verbs. We also discussed which types of verbs can appear on the "other" side of negation: again, in French, all verbs; in English, only auxiliary verbs. We concluded that in French all verbs undergo raising to I, whereas in English only auxiliary verbs do.

Obviously, since French allows all verbs to raise (limiting attention to finite clauses), Affix Hopping is never needed. Since English allows only auxiliary verbs to raise, Affix Hopping is never needed with those; but it is needed for main verbs, which don't raise. We also have to say that in French, not only is Affix Hopping never needed, it's never even possible. Similarly, with auxiliary verbs in English, Affix Hopping is never possible. Somehow, we have to make it true that if V-raising is available, then Affix Hopping won't be allowed. V-raising is preferred to Affix Hopping. This is still very informal. We have to build a theory that entails it.

Finally, there are circumstances in English where V-raising isn't available, because we're dealing with a main verb, and Affix Hopping isn't available either. In those circumstances, and only in those circumstances, *Do*-Support takes place. So, Affix Hopping is preferred to *Do*-Support.

3.5   V-RAISING AND SPLIT I

Let's return to the discrepancy between French and English with respect to which verbs raise. Pollock (1989) proposes a *split-I* hypothesis: I is made up of two categories, Tense and Agreement. We will use the term *I* for a little while longer, and then we will follow Pollock and also break it into Tense and Agreement.

Recall that according to Pollock, French I is morphologically rich and therefore transparent to theta-assignment. That means that structure (82) will always be available in French. In a moment we'll see an argument of Pollock's that not only is structure (82) available, it's the only structure in French.

By saying that I in French is rich, we at least allow structure (82), but, as noted, Pollock goes further and shows that there's no other option in French. In a moment we'll consider why that's the case. On the other hand, in English we already know why there's only one option. Structure (81) will always be ungrammatical; trying to raise a theta-role-assigning verb to I in English ends up violating the Theta-Criterion, because I is always going to be poor. Since structure (81) isn't available at all in English, we have to do something else, namely, Affix Hopping.

I've just codified the fact that there's only one option (configuration (82)) in French by saying that V-raising is preferred to Affix Hopping. However, we have to make that follow from something. If we manage to make it follow from something, then we get a nice state of affairs where each language allows only one possibility.

As discussed earlier, we have to make some fairly strict assumptions about how theta-roles are assigned, in order for Pollock's account to work. One of them has to be the exact negation of certain assumptions made in *LGB*. In *LGB* D-Structure was defined as the level of representation that satisfied the Theta-Criterion. If this is the case, all of Pollock's account collapses. Since the verb that will end up in a configuration like (81) already has assigned its theta-role before it moves, it shouldn't really matter what type of I it adjoins to. So, we have to state that either (1) the Theta-Criterion doesn't really care about D-Structure, or (2) the Theta-Criterion has to be satisfied at D-Structure *and* at some later level of representation, after raising has taken place. Not only do we have to say that it doesn't suffice to satisfy the Theta-Criterion at D-Structure, we also have to say that the trace of the verb isn't a good theta-role assigner, since the relation between *t* and NP in (83), repeated here as (87), is structurally an appropriate configuration for theta-role assignment.

(87)

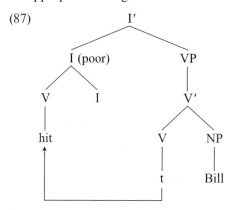

This creates an asymmetry between the traces of verbs and the traces of arguments, as, for example, in the following example involving passive, where the trace of *John* receives the theta-role from the verb (assuming, as we had to a moment ago, that D-Structure satisfaction of the Theta-Criterion doesn't suffice):

(88) John$_i$ was arrested t$_i$

So we need to say here that the trace of a verb *does not* suffice to satisfy the Theta-Criterion, but the trace of an NP *does* suffice to satisfy the Theta-Criterion.

We're led to these conclusions if we want Pollock's account to work. If we want to reject these conclusions, we must seek some other reason why

English main verbs can't raise and French verbs can. Perhaps it's just an irreducible parametric property of language.

As for auxiliary verbs in English, Pollock, and later Chomsky in "Economy," argue that they can raise and must raise because they *don't* have any theta-roles to assign. In a moment we'll explore that aspect of the analysis.

Thus, Pollock's theory offers a reason why French allows all verbs to raise, and why English allows only auxiliary verbs to raise. We don't yet have an answer for the question of why V-raising is preferred to Affix Hopping. Recall the relevant evidence for this "preference" from English and French in (74) and (75), repeated here as (89) and (90).

(89) a.   John often kisses Mary
     b.   *John kisses often Mary

(90) a.   *Jean souvent embrasse Marie
     b.   Jean embrasse souvent Marie

Assuming that adverbs in (89) and (90) are lower than I (e.g., VP-adjoined), the fact that (90a) is impossible in French indicates that V-raising is preferred to Affix Hopping. Let's see how Chomsky tackles this question in "Economy," a further extension of Pollock's proposal.

3.6   VERB MOVEMENT AND ECONOMY: CHOMSKY 1991

3.6.1   Why Raising Is Preferred to Lowering

Chomsky's "Economy" proposal is an extension of the technology I introduced above. Recall the question of where to put the star in the ungrammatical example (73). At first that sounds like a crazy question: it can go anywhere; why does it matter where it goes?

In "Economy" Chomsky argues that it does matter. In particular, if the trace that's created by doing the illicit move is the thing with the star on it, then there might be a chance to fix up the sentence by some later operation. Can we do anything to fix up a sentence that has violated one of these constraints? Later we'll look at Chomsky's argument that it's possible to fix certain violations of the HMC. Right now we're going to look at how he proposes fixing another type of violation. This type of violation involves a kind of constraint based on Fiengo's Proper Binding Condition, which I alluded to earlier but haven't developed yet: A trace, like an anaphor, must be bound. Chomsky formalized the notion of binding in *LGB*. For present purposes binding can be constrained as follows:

(91) A potentially binds B only if A is higher in the tree than B.

The notion "higher in the tree" was formalized by Klima (1964), who called it "in construction with." This is the same geometric relation that Reinhart (1976) called *c-command* (for *category-command*; see note 10). I repeat one definition of it here.

(92) A c-commands B if and only if every X dominating A also
       dominates B.

In a typical subject-object construction, all the categories that dominate the subject also dominate the object. So, the subject c-commands the object. But there are several categories that dominate the object that don't dominate the subject (like V′, VP, I′). So, the object doesn't c-command the subject. When something's moved up, typically it's moved to a c-commanding position. When something's moved down, typically it's moved to a c-commanded position. So, the requirement that something can only move up is the requirement that the moved thing has to c-command its trace.

  Now we get into a question of technology. Chomsky doesn't spell all this out, but roughly he suggests the following. Suppose Affix Hopping applies in English, where I is weak (Chomsky's terms *weak* and *strong* correspond to Pollock's *poor* and *rich*). This creates a trace, but the trace isn't c-commanded by the moved element (as in (93a)). What must happen later in the derivation, then, is that the whole V moves up to the position where the trace is (as in (93b)). Why should this have to happen? Because when we moved I down, we created a starred trace. When we move the whole V complex up into the position of the starred trace, we somehow obliterate the latter.

(93) a.   b.

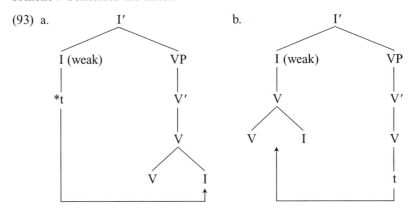

In a moment we'll look into what kind of movement this is. Right now let's say that we have a potential answer for why V-raising is preferred to Affix Hopping. When we do V-raising, we're done. We've gotten the V together with the affix, and the structure is perfectly fine, satisfying the Proper Binding Condition. However, when we do Affix Hopping, we're not done. We have to do something else to fix up the damage that Affix Hopping caused. Chomsky's answer for why V-raising is preferred to Affix Hopping is thus that V-raising results in more *economical* derivations, ones with fewer operations.

One big question arises here. If lowering followed by raising is allowed, then why is it that *John often kisses Mary* is grammatical but *John kisses often Mary* isn't? Let me sketch the theory of grammar in which Chomsky provides an answer. In schema (94) Phonetic Form (PF) is the level of representation most closely connected to "sound," and Logical Form (LF) is the one most closely connected to "meaning."

(94)

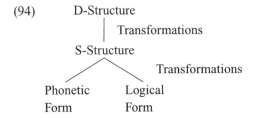

Starting in the mid '70s a lot of work conspired toward the following conclusion: in order to go from S-Structure to LF, we need transformations. I'll give you the flavor of one of the more influential arguments to this effect, due to Huang (1982). Huang was concerned with some of the locality constraints on *Wh*-Movement that Ross had investigated. One such constraint (not actually one of Ross's) was the *Wh-Island Constraint*. Chomsky observed in the early '60s that it's difficult to move a *wh*-phrase out of an embedded question (a question inside another sentence).

(95) *Why do you wonder [what John bought t]?

If (95) were acceptable, it would mean 'What is the reason such that you wonder what John bought for that reason'. Huang showed that in Chinese, where *wh*-phrases don't seem to move, their interpretation apparently obeys the same constraints that the interpretation of moved *wh*-phrases in a language like English seems to obey. So, in Chinese an example like (96) is good but one like (97) is bad on the relevant reading.

(96) Ni   renwei [ta weisheme bu lai]?
      you think   he why   not come
      'Why do you think he didn't come?'

(97) (*) Ni   xiang-zhidao [Lisi weisheme mai-le sheme]?
          you wonder   Lisi why   bought what
      'What is the reason such that you wonder what Lisi bought for that
      reason?'

Hence, this movement constraint seems to obtain even when no "visible"
movement has occurred. The fact that 'why' is obeying movement constraints argues that it really is moving. But this movement is "covert,"
occurring in the mapping from S-Structure to LF, hence not contributing
to pronunciation (i.e., a person who knows Chinese doesn't hear the 'why'
move).

Note that we don't necessarily have to say that there are two different
kinds of transformations. There are just transformations, and they obey
whatever constraints there are. Some of them happen to have pronounce-
able effects, and some of them don't.

To summarize the point: Some elements that don't sound as if they
moved nonetheless behave as if they've moved; hence, we're going to assume they did move. All that's unusual about them is that we can't hear
that they've moved. Why shouldn't we hear that they've moved? Well, if
the grammar includes a component that is "pure" syntax (namely, LF),
that has nothing to do with phonology, and they move in that component,
then we won't hear that they've moved.

Now, recall the apparent contradiction that we faced earlier. One line
of reasoning led to the conclusion that Affix Hopping has to be followed
by re-raising (that's how we answered the question of why V-raising is
preferred to Affix Hopping), but all the standard tests indicate that re-
raising doesn't happen in English.[12] (The verb doesn't occur to the left of
an adverb (recall (89b)), at the beginning of the sentence, or on the other
side of negation.) How can we accept the covert-movement analysis when
all the overt effects we've seen indicate that the verb hasn't re-raised? Now
we have an answer like Huang's. The verb really has re-raised, but it
hasn't re-raised in any component of the grammar that feeds into the
phonology. This suggests that it doesn't matter whether a starred trace
appears in a representation until the derivation is finished. So, we have the
following LF constraint:

(98) Discard a representation that has a starred trace in it at LF.

The fact that a starred trace in the middle of a derivation is inconsequential isn't so unfamiliar. Recall the Stranded Affix Filter. We don't want to say that if an affix is stranded at any point in a derivation, we discard the derivation. If that were so, we'd have to discard all derivations in English because until they're finished, they always have stranded affixes.

The constraint prohibiting stranded affixes may be relevant at the interface between syntax and phonology. Now, we've at least potentially resolved the contradiction. We have a conceptual reason for thinking that when Affix Hopping occurs, re-raising follows. However, since all the overt facts indicate that this raising hasn't occurred in English, we've said that in English the re-raising occurs in the mapping from S-Structure to LF. That still leaves one potential question. We see why we're *allowed* to wait till LF to do the re-raising. But we still don't know why (99) is ungrammatical.

(99) *John reads often books

What if we decide to do the V-raising right away rather than waiting to do it later? Interestingly, in "Economy" Chomsky has nothing to say on this point. He simply assumes that re-raising would have to be an LF phenomenon, but that doesn't follow from anything in the "Economy" theory.[13]

■ *Gutiérrez:* What evidence do we have that when we've done Affix Hopping, re-raising follows?

Lasnik: We'll see directly, when we discuss negation, Chomsky's Huang-type arguments that there are HMC effects in English that are only predicted if re-raising takes place. The crucial one is the ungrammaticality of (100).

(100) *John not left

Chomsky argues that this is explained by the HMC. But, in Chomsky's theory, (100) wouldn't violate the HMC if the V head didn't have to move. ■

3.6.2   Negation and Affix Hopping

Consider the following facts involving negation in English and French:

(101) *John likes not Mary

(102)   Jean (n')aime pas Marie

In English moving the verb across the negation is bad, as in (101), but in French (taking *pas* as the relevant negation) it's good, as in (102). So far, in terms of analysis, we're in pretty good shape, as long as we say that negation starts out higher in the structure than the verb, but lower than I, and if the HMC isn't relevant. But now consider (103).

(103) *John not likes Mary

The ungrammaticality of (103) is a problem for the theory as presented so far. We should have been able to do Affix Hopping, creating a starred trace, and then at LF we should have been able to do the re-raising, fixing up the starred trace. The negation should be totally irrelevant. The question is why the re-raising is bad in this case.

In "Economy" Chomsky argues that (103) violates the HMC. If so, then the question is why (102) doesn't violate it as well. At this point Chomsky suggests a way in which the starred trace created by re-raising in French can be eliminated, but the parallel starred trace in English can't be eliminated.

Let's start looking at the details of Chomsky's account. The way the starred trace is fixed up in French requires a fair amount of technology. Note first that if we want negation to create an HMC violation, then negation has to be a head, as in (104) (certainly reasonable under the extended X-bar theory).

(104) I

          Neg

                 V
                 |
                *t

Recall that Pollock (1989) splits I into two parts: T(ense) and Agr(eement). In "Economy" Chomsky goes further, splitting Agreement into Subject Agreement (Agr$_S$) and Object Agreement (Agr$_O$), the former being located above TP, and the latter below TP and Neg. Adopting this schema, let's reconsider the French example (102), repeated here.

(102) John (n$'$)aime pas Marie

The relevant structure is shown in (105).

(105)

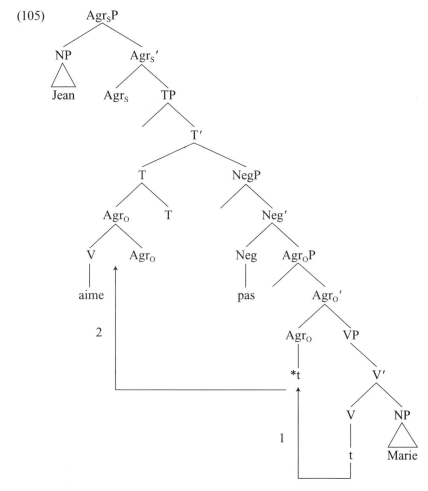

Notice, immediately, that the second step of V-raising, from Agr_O across Neg to T, violates the HMC, so a "bad" trace is created. The question is how the resulting sentence ends up being good. Chomsky's answer is that one of the permissible operations is deletion. We can't just delete elements freely; that is, we can't delete just any element we choose. But we might delete Agr_O. Why might we be tempted to delete Agr_O in LF? Because Agr_O is purely formal (it has no semantic import), so it won't affect the semantic interpretation.

The problem now is that if that derivation is allowed, then we might expect a parallel LF derivation for the English example (103), repeated here, to be allowed.

(103) *John not likes Mary

Let's consider the English situation in more detail. In English, as in French, all the affixes must get together with the verb. But in the case of English main verbs, the affixes must lower to the verb by Affix Hopping.

Let's first look at a grammatical sentence of English with no negation, (106), and its structure in (107).

(106) John likes Mary

(107)

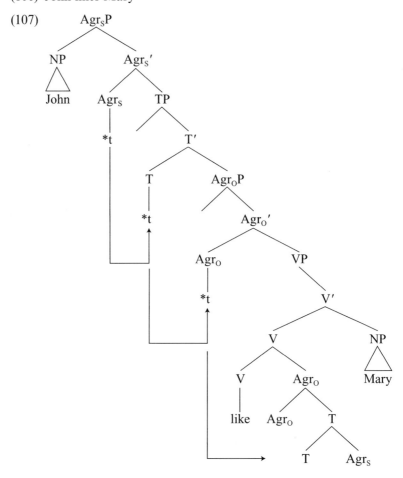

Agr$_S$ lowers to T, creating a starred trace. Then the complex T lowers to Agr$_O$, creating another starred trace. Then the complex Agr$_O$ lowers to V. From the French derivation we know we can delete the trace of Agr$_O$, so by the same reasoning we can delete the trace of Agr$_S$. The question is, how do we fix the starred trace of T? According to Chomsky, we can't delete this trace, because T is semantically important. If we delete T, we'll violate recoverability of deletion. So, instead, we'll eliminate this trace by covertly re-raising. We raise the complex V to Agr$_O$, and then to T, and then to Agr$_S$. I believe Roger Martin was the first to point out that it remains unexplained that even though we can't freely delete the trace of T, we can eliminate the starred trace by superimposing the V (with all of its affixes attached to it) onto T at LF. We will ignore this technical difficulty for now. Also, we will shortly have a reason to reconsider several details of the derivation.

Now let's turn to our negated example, (103). In overt syntax we lower all the affixes, ending up with the structure in (108).

(108)

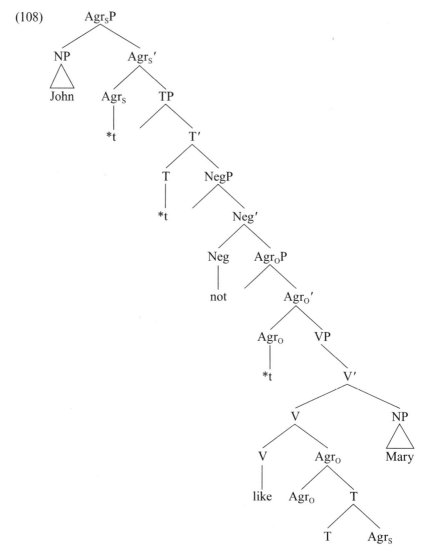

Let's look at what happens with this structure in LF. Because (103) is ungrammatical, we must end up with a starred trace at LF. Further, that starred trace must be in the position of Agr$_O$, since it's the movement from there to T that violates the HMC. In "Economy" Chomsky makes a number of assumptions in order to account for the ungrammaticality of (103).

(109) a. If Agr moves, its trace can be deleted, since it plays no role in LF.

    b. If V moves, its trace cannot be deleted.

    c. Deletion of an element leaves a category lacking features, [e].

    d. Adjunction to [e] (an empty category) is not permitted.

All of these assumptions are explicit in Chomsky's presentation. So, in English, in LF the complex V will try to re-raise to Agr_O, obliterating the starred trace. Then this complex will re-raise to T. Now, what is the category of the trace left behind? If the category is Agr_O and it re-raises to T, then a starred trace is created again, but by (109a) it can be deleted. We thus have to change (109a) into (110).

(110) If Agr moves, its trace *must* be deleted, and *immediately*.

The obligatoriness of this operation and the fact that it must occur immediately don't fit very well with our theory—a conceptual and technical problem, perhaps even an empirical one.

    Putting these questions aside, when we lower Agr_S, its trace will be deleted immediately and we will create an [e]. Next, we will affix-hop T (with Agr_S adjoined to it) onto Agr_O, creating a starred T trace. Then, the whole Agr_O will lower to V; its trace will be deleted immediately, leaving [e].

    Given all these assumptions, the new S-Structure representation of the English example (103) after Affix Hopping is (111).

(111) *S-Structure*

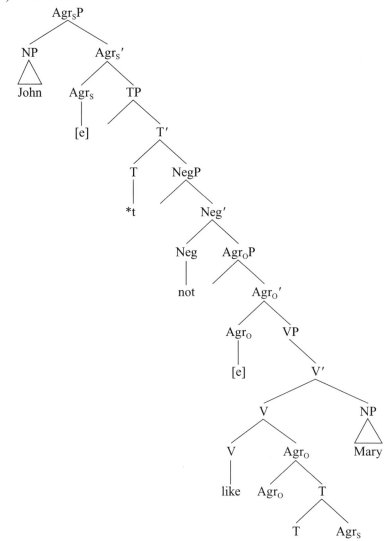

Now we're ready to proceed to the LF component. In LF we'll re-raise
the complex V. Will we adjoin to the [e] (which used to be Agr$_O$)? No.
Recall that one of Chomsky's stipulations, (109d), is that adjuction to [e]
isn't permitted. So, we'll *substitute* the complex V for the [e]. The next step
is to raise the complex V to T in order to eliminate the starred T trace.
But this movement will violate the HMC because it crosses Neg. There-

fore, we'll leave behind a new starred trace, the trace of a V (since in that position a V had substituted for [e]). Finally, the complex T will raise and replace [e] (though it isn't entirely clear why this should be necessary). At this point (103) has the structure in (112) (irrelevant details omitted).

(112) *LF*

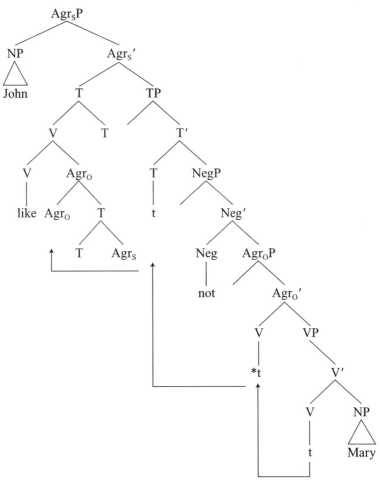

We can't fix up the derivation any further. There's nothing else to re-raise, and the starred trace is the trace of a verb, which we can't delete because it's semantically important, according to Chomsky. In this way we can account for the ungrammaticality of (103). This account works, but very narrowly; it needs a lot of technicalia and, as far as I can tell, is motivated only by the ungrammaticality of (103).

■ *Gutiérrez:*   How can [e] be a category without features?

Lasnik: I suppose that Chomsky has in mind that part of being a category is being an entity. In addition, a category has certain features—the feature of being a verb, a noun, an Agr, and so on. Chomsky seems to be saying that we can take away the entire feature bundle and still have an entity. Let's look at phonology. A phoneme is a bundle of features. If we take away all the features, do we end up with a phoneme with no features, or do we end up with nothing? I'm not sure what phonologists would say about that. On the other hand, we could say, as Chomsky and Halle said in *The Sound Pattern of English* (1968), that there is such a thing as a phoneme that's unmarked for features. A phoneme like that isn't nothing. Maybe we can think of [e] in those terms, in terms of markedness. We can say that [e] is a true syntactic head, but it's unmarked for any features.   ■

■ *Depiante:*   First we had Agr_O, then we had [e], and then we had V, all in the same position. Does that mean that we first had $Agr_O P$, then we had eP, and then we had VP, all in the course of the derivation?

Lasnik: Your question is an important one about the X-bar theory. If we take the X-bar theory to be strictly a property of the base component, it doesn't matter whether we have $Agr_O P$, eP, and VP, since at this point the derivation is long past D-Structure. On the other hand, if we take the X-bar theory to define the notion "syntactic projection," then what we would say is that when Agr_O changes into [e], $Agr_O P$ changes into eP, and when [e] changes into V, eP changes into VP. That's exactly the question of whether the X-bar theory is true of D-Structure only or whether the X-bar theory is true of syntactic structure more generally. Chomsky has taken both positions over the years. For the purposes of this discussion, I'm willing to take the stronger position, that the X-bar theory is true of syntactic structures more generally.

Speaking of levels of representation, one question remains regarding (103). In (103) we've done all the lowering—to keep from violating the Theta-Criterion, you'll recall. First we lowered Agr_S to T, creating an [e], then we lowered T to Agr_O, creating a starred trace, and finally we lowered Agr_O to V, creating an [e]. But then suppose we did the re-raising immediately, not waiting until LF. Why is that bad?   ■

■ *Vukić:*   Wouldn't **John likes not Mary* be ruled out for the same reason that **John not likes Mary* is?

Lasnik: You're right. When we did the derivation of (103), we noticed that we ended up with a starred verb trace. In the derivation of **John *likes not Mary* we'll also end up with a starred verb trace, because we're doing exactly the same movements, except that we're doing them overtly.

We might ask now why the following question is bad:

(113) *Likes John Mary?

Notice that we can't derive this by direct V-raising through all these projections, and then up to C, because that would violate the Theta-Criterion according to Pollock and Chomsky. But lowering and re-raising should be OK. With no intervening heads, there will be no starred traces, V or otherwise. Chomsky has suggested that interrogative C is an affix in English-type languages. Given that suggestion, the problem boils down to this: why can auxiliaries, but not "true" verbs, raise to that affix to support it? In Chomsky's "Economy" terms, we're pretty much forced to say that the interrogative affix in English is theta-opaque and so (113) should be a violation of the Theta-Criterion.   ∎

3.6.3 *Do*-Support

Chomsky (1991) talks around the issue of *Do*-Support but doesn't exactly address it. He talks about what properties *Do*-Support will have to have with respect to economy but doesn't actually formulate the rule. As far as I can tell, the best statement of *Do*-Support is still something like the one in *LSLT*.

In "Economy" Chomsky does offer a proposal about why *Do*-Support is a last resort. He says that V-raising and Affix Hopping are instances of Move Alpha ("Move anything anywhere, subject to general constraints"). *Do*-Support is an operation that adjoins *do* to some head (we'll specify which one later). The claim is that V-raising and Affix Hopping are instantiations of a universal process, movement, whereas *Do*-Support is an English-particular process. *Do*-Support is a last resort because it's not a universal operation. In "Economy" Chomsky claims that universal operations always apply first, if they can. Language-particular operations take place only as a last resort. The only time *Do*-Support will have a chance to apply is when straight raising is unavailable (with main verbs) and when Affix Hopping followed by re-raising is unavailable (as happens in negative sentences).

Notice that even in negative sentences we aren't obviously going to have any trouble associating Agr_O with the verb. We'll have trouble associating Agr_S and T with the verb, when we try to do the re-raising. But Agr_O is so close to the verb, we won't have any trouble with it. That also goes along with the following suggestion: when a sentence includes both auxiliary verbs and a main verb, Agr$_S$ and T go with the auxiliary verb (that part is really right out of *Syntactic Structures*) and Agr$_O$ goes with the main verb.

Here, then, is a concrete proposal for the insertion of *do* in a sentence like *John does not like Mary*. We adjoin *do* to T; then we move the complex T and adjoin it to Agr$_S$, as shown in (114) (irrelevant details aside).

(114)

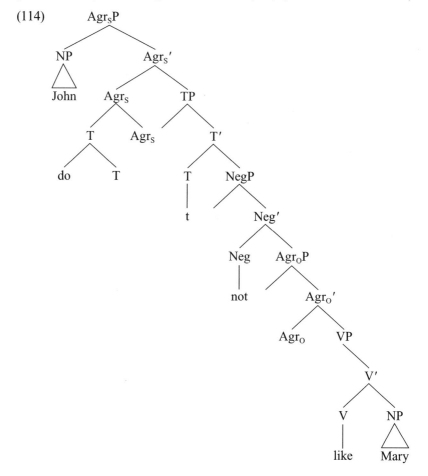

3.6.4 Deletions

It's time for me to emphasize that in this theory the only time we can do movement is when it's driven by something; we can't just move things gratuitously. That's the guiding metaphor in this and other approaches involving economic considerations. What could drive movement? For example, an affix. Chomsky has also proposed that other sorts of formal features can drive movement. There might be features that must be satisfied. A head with some formal feature might be able to be satisfied only if something gets close enough to it. Consider as one example the Agr$_S$ head. The features of this head can only be satisfied if there's a subject close to it. To put it the other way around, no matter where the subject starts, it has to get close to the Agr$_S$ head because the formal features of the Agr$_S$ head are agreement features. They somehow have to agree with something.

So, among other things, stranded affixes and agreement features drive movement. The next question is, what drives deletion? Chomsky's theory includes the notion of *chain*: a chain consists of an item that moves and all of its traces, as schematized in (115).

(115) X, t(x), t(x), t(x)

Chomsky proposes that a chain might be *uniform* or *nonuniform*. A chain is uniform if X and all of its traces are the same with respect to being head positions, being XP argument-type positions (*A-positions*), or being XP nonargument-type positions (*Ā-positions*). A chain is nonuniform if X and all of its traces are not the same with respect to being head, A-, or Ā-positions.

Now, here's the punch line of Chomsky's proposal, crucial to his explanation of a range of locality effects including *Wh*-Movement. A uniform chain is a *legitimate* LF object (even if it has a starred trace in it). In line with the general economy metaphor that there always has to be a reason for doing an operation, deletion is allowed only to turn an illegitimate LF object into a legitimate LF object.

However, by this reasoning, it shouldn't be possible to delete the trace of Agr$_O$, given that it's part of a legitimate LF object, a uniform head chain. This is an apparent internal inconsistency within "Economy."

3.7 THE MINIMALIST APPROACH TO VERBAL MORPHOLOGY: CHOMSKY 1993

3.7.1 Checking Theory

The fundamental difference between "Economy" (Chomsky 1991) and "A Minimalist Program for Linguistic Theory" (Chomsky 1993) (hereafter "A Minimalist Program") is that the latter makes no crucial use of affixes. Let's put this into a conceptual setting and then see what the consequences are.

In the '50s and early '60s, transformations did "everything." Some connected inflectional morphemes with verbs (*leave + past = left*). Others attached derivational morphemes to verbs (*destroy + tion = destruction*); these were the so-called nominalizing transformations. In "Remarks on Nominalization" Chomsky argued that this was wrong. He put forward the *Lexicalist Hypothesis*, which says that transformations perform only inflectional morphology, not derivational morphology. In this view *destruction* is in the lexicon, but *destroyed* still isn't. Chomsky pointed out that not all verbs nominalize, but all verbs have a past tense form. In addition, the verbs that nominalize do it in vastly different ways. Chomsky also observed that the semantics of inflectional morphology is completely transparent; if we know the meaning of a verb, we know the meaning of its past tense. Not so for derivational morphology.

In "A Minimalist Program" Chomsky goes even further. He says that even inflectional morphology isn't performed transformationally, a claim we can call the *Strict Lexicalist Hypothesis*. Given that hypothesis, Chomsky concludes that the functional heads (Agr$_S$, T, Agr$_O$) aren't affixes. Words are pulled out of the lexicon already in their final shape, abstracting away from phonological rules.

One immediate virtue of this theory is that lowering and re-raising won't be an issue, because there won't be any lowering. We were doing the lowering because we had affixes that would otherwise be stranded. But, if there are no affixes, there are no stranded affixes, so lowering is no longer an issue. That's an apparent step forward: we no longer have complicated lowering and re-raising derivations.

But then, what's the difference between French and English? Maybe we can just stop at this point and say the theory is so elegant that we don't care anymore whether we explain the differences between English and French. That's not what Chomsky says in "A Minimalist Program" (though that's what he essentially says in "Categories and Transformations" (1995), if I understand that work correctly).

Conceptually speaking, there are two ways to think about inflectional morphology. One is the traditional generative way: a stem and an affix get together by means of a transformation that creates a word. The other way is this: the word is already complete in the lexicon, but it somehow has to be "certified." Sometimes linguists describe the first theory by saying that the affix has to be "assigned" to the stem, and the second theory by saying that the affix is already part of the stem but it has to be "checked." In "A Minimalist Program" Chomsky argues that the checking theory gives a nicer account of the differences between English and French than the assignment theory does.

Let's look at French first. In "A Minimalist Program" Chomsky argues that the finite verb is a bundle of features including tense and agreement features. Chomsky calls the latter *phi-features* (person, gender, number). These features are in the verb all along; they won't be assigned by a transformation. The features on the verb have to be checked against the features in the Agr_S, T, and Agr_O heads, to guarantee a match. How are these features checked? They're checked in a very local relation, the head-to-head relation. The verb raises to Agr_O to check some of its features, then to T, and then to Agr_S. The process is the same for both English and French. Why, then, is the verb overtly higher in French than in English? Recall the principle Procrastinate, which says this:

(116) *Procrastinate*
     Wait until LF to do any operations if at all possible.

Chomsky claims that the difference between French and English depends on Procrastinate. It doesn't matter when the features are "certified," as long as it's done by the time the derivation reaches LF. Simple English sentences work fine: in English, features can be checked at any time, so Procrastinate demands that they not be checked until LF. The issue of lowering and re-raising doesn't arise; everything is taken care of by raising in the covert component.

But now we've ruled out French. We know that in French, raising simply can't be put off. The verb is always to the left of the adverb, to the left of negation, and so on. Raising—that is, checking of relevant features—has to happen overtly. In this framework, as in more recent developments of it, that is irreducible. Linguists sometimes pretend it can be deduced from something else by restating it in a technological fashion, but no one has come close to explaining it. One popular technological translation is as follows: Agr_S, T, and Agr_O contain certain features that are "strong" in French but "weak" in English. In this respect, Chomsky makes the following proposal:

(117) An unchecked strong feature is an illegitimate PF object.[14]

In French, if the verb doesn't raise until LF, the strong features in Agr_S, T, and Agr_O remain unchecked overtly; they survive into PF and are

illegitimate at the PF level. In both English and French, verbs are pulled out of the lexicon fully inflected, complete with tense and phi-features. The LF structures in French and English will be exactly the same in the checking theory, which was not the case for the LF structures in French and English in the "Economy" theory (cf. the French LF structure corresponding to (107) and the English LF structure in (112)). For example, the LF structure of both English (118a) and French (118b) is the one shown in (119).

(118) a. John likes Mary
      b. Jean aime Marie

(119) *LF*

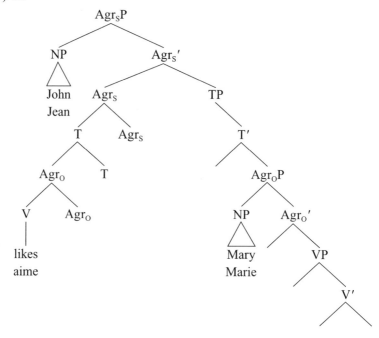

That's the essence of the proposals in "A Minimalist Program." In English everything stays low because of Procrastinate; the verb eventually ends up high, but we can't hear it there, because the raising is done at LF. In French Procrastinate still wants the raising process to wait, but waiting results in an illegitimate PF object, because the strong features remain unchecked overtly. Like any version of Procrastinate, this one still has a computationally complex look-ahead property. At the point when raising takes place, it's not fixing up any immediate violation; instead, it's taking place so that a violation won't turn up 19 steps down the road.[15]

A couple of questions remain. Why do *have* and *be* raise overtly in English? Here's the answer Chomsky gives in "A Minimalist Program." He talks about *have* and *be*, ignoring modals, and proposes (120).

(120) *Have* and *be* are semantically vacuous; therefore, they are invisible for operations in the LF component.

We then continue to assume (121).

(121) An unchecked feature (of any sort) is an illegitimate LF object.

This is why French and English LF structures end up looking identical. Languages differ with regard to when they check their features, but all features have to be checked eventually. So, in deriving (122), we pull *is* from the lexicon.

(122) John is a student

All the features in Agr_S, T, and Agr_O need to be checked. One would think they wouldn't be checked overtly because of Procrastinate, but if we wait until LF, we won't be able to check them at all, because *is* is semantically vacuous, hence invisible for operations in LF. We then would end up with an illegitimate structure at LF. Therefore, we must raise *is* overtly, to be able to check the features of Agr_S, T, and Agr_O.

In sum: If a language has strong features on the functional heads T or Agr, raising always takes place overtly. If a language has weak features on functional heads, main verbs never raise overtly, but auxiliary verbs always raise overtly, because if they wait too long, they lose their chance to raise at all, and the functional heads end up with unchecked features.

3.7.2 Two Problems

Here's a big question. How does this theory account for the ungrammaticality of (123)?

(123) a. *John left not
      b. *John not left

Surprisingly, since they were central in "Economy," in "A Minimalist Program" Chomsky doesn't mention these examples. In the latter theory (123a) would perhaps violate Procrastinate, but (123b) would then be incorrectly predicted to be good. There's no way that I can see within this theory to rule out (123b). The correct derivation of (123b) would be precisely identical to the overt derivations of the corresponding French example. This is a major problem, I believe.

In addition, this theory faces a problem of a more conceptual nature, having to do with (120), the claim that *have* and *be* are "invisible" in LF because of their semantic vacuity. When people hear this claim, they tend to accept it, seduced by the name of the LF component, Logical Form, which sounds like it's semantics. But when you articulate the theories, LF isn't semantics, it's syntax. Move Alpha applies between D-Structure and S-Structure and between S-Structure and LF, the only difference being whether the results are audible or not. Where is there room in a theory like that to say something like (120)? In fact, the thrust of all of Chomsky's work since the 1950s is that syntactic operations are blind to semantics. We take something of the right type and move it to a position of the right type; we never care about its meaning. There's a classic argument, first presented by Bresnan (1972), that no language has a rule of "*Red* Extraposition," which would take any word or phrase that includes the concept of redness, without caring whether it's an adjective, a verb, or a noun, and move it to the end of the sentence. That's a strong argument that transformations are blind to semantic properties. But such a theory provides no obvious way of saying something like (120).

On the more empirical level, it seems that certain occurrences of *have* and even of *be* do have some meaning. This theory would predict that a *have* or a *be* that has some meaning should not be allowed to raise overtly because Procrastinate would say to wait. But that might not be true. For example, there's no obvious semantic difference between (124a) and (124b). But *is* raises, as shown in (125), and *exists* doesn't, as shown in (126).

(124) a. There is a solution
     b. There exists a solution

(125) a. Is there a solution?
     b. There is not a solution

(126) a. *Exists there a solution?
     b. *There exists not a solution

Another argument against (120) comes from the Swedish examples in (127). In Swedish, main verbs seem to remain in situ in embedded sentences. Swedish allows the equivalent of *John not left*, with no *Do*-Support and no raising. Chomsky's theory in "A Minimalist Program" predicts that the equivalents of *have* and *be* in other languages have to raise; but in

Swedish they don't raise. If we assume that Swedish is like any other language in requiring all the features on functional heads to be checked, then (120) must be false.

(127) a. ... om   hon inte ofte har sett honom
                  whether she not often has seen him
       b. *... om hon har inte ofte sett honom
       c. *... om hon inte har ofte sett honom

In what follows we'll try to deal with the first of the above problems, the ungrammaticality of (123b). The account I will present is essentially the one I gave in Lasnik 1995, which draws on the insight captured in the *Syntactic Structures* framework.

3.8 *SYNTACTIC STRUCTURES* REVIVED: LASNIK 1995

3.8.1 A "Lexicalist" versus "Bare" Distinction

Let's again look at the problematic sentences in (123).

(123) a. *John left not
       b. *John not left

These were two of the major cases that Chomsky dealt with in *Syntactic Structures* and *LSLT*, as well as in "Economy." In "Economy" he deals with it in a very different way than in the '50s. In the '50s the core notion involved in explaining facts like these was *linear adjacency*. In the "Economy" approach Chomsky still incorporates Affix Hopping and a sort of notion of adjacency, but with two differences. One, the adjacency isn't linear. Instead, it's *hierarchical adjacency*, the HMC: an element can't skip a head by moving across it. Two, the adjacency isn't relevant to the lowering operations at all. It's relevant to the hypothesized LF re-raising operation.

Chomsky's system that includes the adjacency constraint in the form of the HMC handles the problem, but only barely, since there's only one fact to explain—(103)—and about five stipulations to account for it. To say that an Agr trace can be deleted may not be a stipulation. To say that it *must* be deleted borders on a stipulation. To say it must be deleted *immediately* is clearly a stipulation. Also, to say that deletion means creation of a peculiar "empty category" is a sort of stipulation. To say that adjunction to this "empty category" is prohibited is a stipulation. All those stipulations are made to account for just that one fact. If it weren't for that fact, we could dispense with all those stipulations and restate French in a much simpler way.

The theory in "A Minimalist Program" doesn't handle the problem at all. All of the technicalities of the "Economy" theory account for crucial differences between the relevant French structures and the relevant English structures. But the virtue of the theory in "A Minimalist Program," according to Chomsky, is that there's no difference between the French structures and the English structures. Recall that the "Economy" English structure involves lowering operations and the ensuing havoc, whereas in French no lowering precedes raising, so the structures in the two languages are very different. Now, in the analysis developed in "A Minimalist Program," lowering doesn't precede raising in any language. The structures are always identical crosslinguistically. We can no longer use the HMC to account for the difference between languages. Another way of saying this is that if the HMC is going to throw out a particular kind of example in some languages, it's going to throw it out in all languages: there's no way to make a distinction any more. None.

What can we do? We can go back to the "Economy" theory, although with that theory we have to graft on some technology that doesn't fit very naturally. Or, and this is the approach I finally took when I was researching this topic in the early 1990s, we should go back to something like the *Syntactic Structures* idea. The core intuition is the following. What's relevant in (123b) *is* linear adjacency. The reason *John not left* is ungrammatical is that there's an affix *past* and there's a bare verb *leave*, which want to get together; the way they get together is that the affix attaches to the verb, and that attachment process demands adjacency—which doesn't obtain in (123b).

Recall that we ran into trouble with (123b) in English, but we didn't run into such trouble with French: French really worked out nicely. Let's then accept the analysis for French. In French all verbs are "lexicalist." That is, they aren't constructed syntactically or in any other way; rather, they're introduced with all their phi-features on them, which they later check. Further, French I (in the non-split-I framework that I'll use for this part of the discussion, for simplicity) has some strong V-features. In English, of course, we have to distinguish main and auxiliary verbs.[16] What's the simplest thing we can say about auxiliaries? They behave like all verbs in French; that is, they're "lexicalist." Further, just like in French, "I" has (some) strong V-features. Now, we're not sure what positive thing we're going to say about main verbs, but we know what negative thing we're going to say. Recall that the theory in "A Minimalist Program" collapses because English main verbs are considered "lexicalist." Let's now say that English main verbs are *not* "lexicalist." We then have to figure out what they *are*.

At this point we've got to make one proviso. Either we have to accept something like Chomsky's technology in addition to the HMC for French and for English auxiliary verbs, or we have to say there's no such thing as the HMC or that it's inoperative here. We've seen that the HMC alone won't handle facts about negation: we must allow V-raising across negation.

We've said that English main verbs aren't "lexicalist." It's not necessarily a pure two-way distinction—either "lexicalist" (as in "A Minimalist Program") or something else—but let's treat it as such right now. Let's say the only alternative to being "lexicalist" is the *Syntactic Structures* option: main verbs are bare and then they pick up affixal material.

If that's all we've said, then we're still in trouble, as (128) shows.

(128)

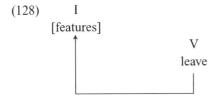

Since the verb is bare, it has no features to be checked against the features in I, which will therefore remain unchecked. Obviously, we also have to introduce the concomitant *Syntactic Structures* machinery. If we're introducing bare verbs that will eventually turn into, say, finite verbs, we've got to introduce *finiteness* as an affix in English. Let's say that in French "I" is "*featural*," that is, not an affix, but a bundle of abstract features that have to be checked. In English we also want "I" to be "featural": that's how we derive *John is not singing*. But if that's all we say, then English should be just like French at best. On the other hand, we know the obvious way to derive *John left* if main verbs are bare—we decided that they must be, or we run into the **John not left* problem again. So, we have to add one more possibility for English "I": it can be affixal too. We now have a hybrid theory, combining elements of the very old one and the more modern one.

Let me begin to generalize these two possibilities. My proposal looks like a complication but I think it's a simplification, in the sense that more general is simpler (as I've repeatedly said, phonologists have known that for generations). If we say that in English "I" can be "featural" *or* affixal, why don't we say that in French "I" is also "featural" *or* affixal? When we're building a tree, we can pull a "featural" I out of the lexicon, or we can pull out an affixal I, a free choice.

3.8.2 Sample Derivations

Let's look at some possible trees, first without negation. Suppose we're trying to construct a French sentence, and we pull a verb out of the lexicon. French verbs are "lexicalist" (our only stipulation), so there's no possibility of pulling out a bare verb. Each verb has a bundle of inflectional features $[F_1, F_2, F_3, \ldots]$. Now, there are two principal ways we can proceed to build the tree. One way involves I with the matching features $[F_1, F_2, F_3, \ldots]$. The verb will raise and the features will be checked, as in (129).

(129)

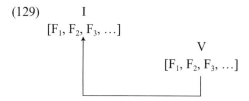

The other way, which we're now permitting, involves I with an affix and a verb with the features $[F_1, F_2, F_3, \ldots]$, as illustrated in (130).

(130)   I
    [affix]
             V
        $[F_1, F_2, F_3, \ldots]$

The verb won't raise to I—raising won't be driven by V-features (strong or otherwise), since there aren't any in I. The affix in I might try to get together with the verb, but obviously some kind of constraint is at work here: an inflectional affix can get together with a bare stem, but it can't get together with something that already has inflection in it. We can add an affix to, say, *leave* but not to *left*. One can imagine various ways of building that intuition into a theoretical principle. Arguably, because the verb and the affix can't get together, two violations will occur without any further stipulation. First, the verbal features in (130) won't get checked, which, as Chomsky argues, is an LF violation. Second, the affix in I will be a stranded affix, since there's no appropriate host for it—a PF violation.

Notice what all this means: we don't need to preclude the possibility that I in French is affixal. That would be redundant; the relevant instances are ruled out independently, as we've just seen.

The above considerations cover all of the French cases. Now let's look at the English cases, which are more interesting. In French there is never overt evidence for the affixal I. But in English there is such evidence. English truly makes use of both possibilities, so we need to look at all the combinations.

The structure in (129), repeated here, with the "featural" I and the "lexicalist" verb, arises for English, but only for auxiliary verbs.

(129)

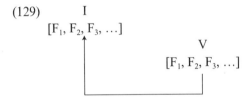

Main verbs will never appear in this particular structure, because there are no main verbs that are "featural" (according to our stipulation).

The structure in (130) could also imaginably arise for English auxiliary verbs; but we know that this structure can't lead to any good outcome, since it's the same structure we just excluded for French. It doesn't matter here which language we're considering: the same kind of violations (stranded affix, unchecked features) will occur in English as in French. Again, we need no additional stipulation to rule out this possibility.

There are two other logically possible cases to consider. One case is shown in (131) (where, for the moment, the bare stem is indicated as V+).

(131)   I
         [affix]
                 V+

In (131) the affix gets together nicely with the bare verb, producing an inflected verb form. Now let's see exactly how they get together. They don't get together by V-raising, since if they did, we would hear the verb "on the other side of" various elements, such as negation. That doesn't happen in English. Do they get together by I-lowering? That's conceivable, but I don't think it's necessary. To talk about the combining of the affix and the bare verb as a lowering operation is to talk about it as part of syntax, a syntactic operation. But as soon as we look at the negative sentences, we'll see that we need an *adjacency* stipulation for the operation, just like in *Syntactic Structures*. It's virtually unheard of for operations that are clearly syntactic to care about linear adjacency (see also section 2.7.7). So I would want to argue, as I suggested in a footnote in Lasnik 1981 (based on an idea of Joseph Kupin's), that it isn't a true syntactic operation, but a sort of "interface" operation between syntax and morphology.

With that in mind, the last case to look at is the one already mentioned in (128). This case is schematized in (132).

(132)   I
       $[F_1, F_2, F_3, \ldots]$
                    V+

(132) represents a case of "featural" I, together with the bare stem. As we already know, this possibility will be ruled out because the features of I will remain unchecked.

One other kind of possibility arises for English as well. We've been distinguishing auxiliary and main verbs in English, in a categorical, not relational, sense. That's too strong an assumption, just like it's too strong an assumption to say that only main verbs occur bare in English. Consider the following relevant cases discussed in *Syntactic Structures*:

(133) He seems to *be* ill

(134) It must *be* raining

Recall that according to the analysis in *Syntactic Structures* verbs following modals must be in the bare form (a claim internal to the theory allowing phonologically null affixes). The point is that both main verbs *and* auxiliary verbs can occur bare in English, as (133) and (134) show. On the one hand, that gets rid of a stipulation in the lexicon. On the other hand, it's going to cause a problem, as we will now see.

So in the cases considered above we could, in principle, have a bare main verb or a bare auxiliary verb; it seems that the latter ought to exist. In (130) and (132) it doesn't matter whether the verb is main or auxiliary; the features won't get checked. Our theory has to allow an affixal I, or we can't derive *John left*. Likewise, it has to allow bare auxiliaries, or we can't derive (133)–(134). So, this combination is forced upon us by the theory.

The trouble it could cause is that if we put negation between the I and the bare stem in (131), as in (135), there shouldn't be any way to get the inflection together with the auxiliary.

(135)   I

[affix]

      not

          V+

But if there's no way to get the inflection together with the auxiliary, then we should get *Do*-Support, which I take to be simply the pronunciation of a bare affix when it's "stranded." So, in fact, we should expect the following type of example:

(136) *It does not be raining

It's very hard to prevent (136), which is the one significant problem I know of facing the hybrid approach. Somehow, the possibility of the "lexicalist" *It is not raining* should preclude (136), rather in the way the existence of an irregular verb form (e.g., *brought*) precludes the existence of the corresponding regular form (e.g., *bringed*). But I don't see how to make this precise at the moment.

3.8.3 Negative Sentences

Abstracting away from the problem of (136), let's look at more familiar kinds of negative sentences and make sure our theory can handle them correctly. What are the possibilities for trying to generate these?

In dealing with negative sentences, we've got to try one or the other kind of I: "featural" or affixal. The "featural" one won't work at all: the features can't get checked. Let's therefore stick with the affixal one, as in (137).

(137) John

        I

     [affix]

       not

         leave

Leave can't raise, not because of the HMC (none of the grammatical sentences we've looked at obeyed the HMC), but because, according to Chomsky, movement is driven by *features*. In (137) neither I nor *leave* has any features to be checked by raising; therefore, no movement takes place.

There's one other derivation to consider, one involving Affix Hopping. If Affix Hopping could take place, we could possibly derive *John not left*. But Affix Hopping demands adjacency, and the affix in I isn't adjacent to its potential host, *leave*. Therefore, Affix Hopping isn't possible either.

Is there anything we can do? We can salvage the stranded affix just the way Chomsky did in *Syntactic Structures*: by spelling it out as a form of *do*. The result is *John does not leave* or *John did not leave*, depending on the tense property of I.[17]

So, that's one way we can integrate both affixation and checking into the theory. The only stipulation is, again, that French verbs are "lexicalist" whereas English main verbs are bare.

3.8.4   Imperatives

Finally, let's take a look at imperatives, in light of the above considerations. Consider the following typical imperative:

(138) Leave!

On initial inspection it's hard to tell exactly what *leave* in (138) is; it might be bare, or it might be the second person present. We know that the second person present ending in English is null.

How do we find out whether there's a real affix in the second person present form? The test involves negative imperatives where *Do*-Support (which supports the affix) takes place.

(139) a. Don't leave!
       b. Do not leave!

If we accept Chomsky's parallel argument in *Syntactic Structures*, we'll conclude that imperative sentences do involve an affix. As far as we can tell so far, this could be the second person present affix.

But there's one test that shows that this affix is *not* the second person present affix in English. *Be* is the only verb in English whose second person present (*are*) doesn't sound like its infinitive form. Obviously in relevant counterparts of (138) *be* occurs, not *are*.

(140) *Are kind!/Be kind!

It might seem like a paradox: I've just proved that there's an affix in (139), but I've also proved that it's not the second person present. But it's not a paradox; we've simply found another affix. Let's call it an *imperative affix*. So, imperative sentences have an I. Furthermore, it's an affixal one that triggers *Do*-Support; that is, it doesn't trigger raising. Now consider the following cases:

(141) a. Don't be foolish!
       b. Do not be foolish!

(142) a. *Ben't foolish!
       b. *Be not foolish!

Since raising doesn't take place, we're not dealing with the "lexicalist" form for imperatives or a "featural" I. We're presumably dealing with a *bare* verb and an *affixal* I, as in (143).

(143)   I
          [affix]
       [imperative]

                      not

                      V+
                      be

Merging of the imperative affix and the bare stem is blocked by the intervening negation, as illustrated by the following examples:

(144) a. *Not leave!
       b. *Not be foolish!

The paradigm is now complete.

3.8.5 VP-Ellipsis

Some very interesting facts about VP-ellipsis in English, first discussed by Warner (1986), receive a nice account under the hybrid morphological theory. Usually VP-ellipsis can ignore differences in form between an antecedent verb and an elided one. (145) is surely derived from (146) and not from (147).

(145)   John slept, and Mary will too

(146)   John slept, and Mary will sleep too

(147)   *John slept, and Mary will slept too

So the infinitive *sleep* can delete under identity with the finite *slept*. Present tense behaves like past tense.

(148) Mary plays golf, and John should too

(149) Mary plays golf, and John should play golf too

These facts had been recognized for some time. What Warner noticed is that this kind of "sloppy" identity doesn't work for auxiliary verbs.

(150) *John was here, and Mary will too

(151) John was here, and Mary will be here too

Was can't antecede *be*, even though *slept* can antecede *sleep* and *plays* can antecede *play*. A similar effect shows up with auxiliary *have*, though it's possibly more subtle.

(152) John has left, but Mary shouldn't

(153) John has left, but Mary shouldn't have left

(152) can't mean (153); it can only mean (154).

(154) John has left, but Mary shouldn't leave

Just as *was* can't antecede *be*, auxiliary *has* can't antecede *have*. It seems as if inflected main verbs can be treated as if they're bare, for the purposes of identity deletion, but auxiliary verbs can't.[18]

Remember now how the hybrid account of English verbal morphology works. Main verbs are introduced bare, and they later get together with affixes. Auxiliary verbs are introduced fully inflected. This means that through most of the derivation, *slept*, for example, is strictly identical to *sleep*. On the other hand, *was* is never identical to *be*. If the ellipsis process can look at the representation of *slept* before Affix Hopping, it can match it up with *sleep*. But no matter where in the derivation it looks, it will never find a way to match *was* up with *be*.

The analysis of this peculiar ellipsis paradigm converges with the analysis of the facts about the distribution of negation in English that we examined earlier. We have further evidence, then, that *Syntactic Structures* was basically correct, with just one limitation: auxiliary verbs are "lexicalist." If this claim is on the right track, one of my justifications at the outset for looking at such outdated material is fulfilled: sometimes long-abandoned analyses are actually correct. It wouldn't be a bad idea to periodically root through other classics of the field to see if more dinosaurs are worth bringing back to life.

Notes

Introduction

1. Like this book, *Syntactic Structures* began its life as lecture notes. You will find it useful, as you proceed through the book, to have *Syntactic Structures* at hand.

Chapter 1

1. NP is just one symbol, not two, even though it is written with two letters, and similarly for VP. NP *ought* to be somehow based on N, but in this model it is not, a problem remedied in Chomsky 1970.

2. Recall that the definition of derivation says that we have to replace *exactly one symbol* in each line. In this case we replaced NP, but we had two choices: we could have replaced VP instead. We will see that this choice ultimately has no effect on the output: the alternative derivations are "equivalent."

3. It is crucial here that we rewrite VP as V S and not as V; otherwise, we will not be able to generate the sentence (53a).

4. In our discussion of trees, we will adopt the standard terminology of constituent analysis; in particular, we will say that one node *dominates* (is above) the other (e.g., the lower S in (63) dominates NP, N, *Mary*, VP, V, and *sings*, and immediately dominates NP and VP). We will also use "kinship" terms to describe other relations between nodes in the tree: that is, a node that immediately dominates another is called its *mother*, and the node that it dominates a *daughter*. Two nodes with the same mother are called *sisters*.

5. This is the first step that differs from the previous derivation.

6. From now on I will simply say *PS tree*, always implying a collapsed one, unless otherwise indicated.

7. I adopt the conventional assumptions of semantic compositionality: that syntactic constituent structure roughly corresponds to semantic constituent structure.

8. We will see later what to do in cases where superficially there is no auxiliary. Positing that there is an auxiliary in cases where there seems to be none will solve

the problem of why it is that speakers feel that *John will win. Will John win?* and *John won. Did John win?* are part of the same paradigm.

9. We will see more on this later.

10. Here there is no direct evidence.

Chapter 2

1. We also still have to determine what C is.

2. Harris's work on transformations began in the late 1940s and appeared in print as Harris 1952 and Harris 1957.

3. In section 2.3.2.1 I will discuss the formal nature of adjunction in more detail.

4. The present form of *will, will s*, is realized as *will*.

5. For ease of exposition I have labeled the four cases in this SA as *a., b., c.,* and *d.* Note that in *Syntactic Structures* the third term in the SA is *V* ... This means 'V followed by anything at all'; it's equivalent to *V* + *X* or *V X*. Chomsky's notation is somewhat inconsistent on this point.

6. Keep in mind that this third person present *s* morpheme is abstract, usually, but not always, being realized as [s] (or [z] or [əz]) by regular phonological rules.

7. Morphophonemics, or phonology, is the component of the grammar responsible for relating the structure of a word to its pronunciation.

8. *Left* adjunction would be the mirror image.

9. We will return to Chomsky's argument that there is in fact an affix in this case.

10. We will return to this point in more detail later on.

11. Recall that *s* is abstract, so the fact that it is not phonetically realized here is of no direct import.

12. There is a question of potential technical interest here. Obviously Affix Hopping takes place twice in (73). Does it happen all at once? If not, does it happen first in one place and then in the other, and if so, is there an algorithm that specifies how it happens? In phonology of the type developed in *The Sound Pattern of English* (Chomsky and Halle 1968), this is an important question. Given a phonological rule that is applicable several places in a word, does it apply all at once, or does it iterate from left to right, or does it iterate from right to left? We will return to this later.

13. In *Syntactic Structures* two rules are labeled T21. I call the first of them T21a, and the second T21b.

14. With the usual proviso about the term "Af" (see above).

15. Like X and Y, Z and W are string variables.

16. We started with an initial PM (100), from which we derived (101), from which we further derived (104). Recall a point I made early on: transformations fundamentally are defined on PMs. The result of applying a transformation must be formally like a PM; if it weren't, we would never be able to get sequences of transformations. We now see this formal idea instantiated.

17. Recall that this isn't truly an SA, since "Af" and "v" aren't symbols of the grammar. Rather, this is an abbreviation for 20 SAs.

18. Or maybe A-*under*-A if Vukić's earlier intuition about the structures at issue is right.

19. This account of negative questions contrasts sharply with the *Syntactic Structures* account of passive sentences. Passive sentences as described there differ from actives in three ways: the verb carries (1) passive morphology: *be en*; (2) the understood object occurs in subject position; (3) the understood subject occurs at the end of the VP, with *by*. The Passive Transformation simply stipulates all three of these properties. Later, in "Remarks on Nominalization" (1970), Chomsky began to develop a much more successful account, "modular" in the way that the *Syntactic Structures* account of negative questions is modular.

20. As usual, Z and W are string variables, like X and Y.

21. The problem that will arise here will arise in the same way with auxiliary *be* (and auxiliary *have* as well).

22. There is one immediate technical problem with extending the V → *be* proposal to auxiliary *be*. But it is a problem that is so pervasive in the whole theory that we can put it aside here. The problem is, how do we get the right cooccurrence relation between *be* and *ing* and between *have* and *en* if the PS rule for Aux is now something like this: $Aux \rightarrow C\ (M)\ (V + en)\ (V + ing)$?

This problem is one reason why Chomsky did not say that *be* is a V. There is a similar difficulty in distinguishing between transitive and intransitive verbs. Whatever way we find to distinguish transitives from intransitives might, as a consequence, solve this problem too. We ultimately need some way of distinguishing one type of verb from another, regardless. In *Aspects* Chomsky introduced "subcategorization" and "selection" to address this range of problems. I will return to this issue.

23. $N!$ ("N factorial") means $N \times (N - 1) \times (N - 2) \times \cdots \times 2 \times 1$.

24. Alternatively, we might ultimately conclude that syntactic rules do not care about adjacency at all, in which case we would simply disallow this hypothesized adjacency symbol. In section 3.8 we will see that the adjacency requirement is real, but that the process requiring it is not necessarily a syntactic transformation.

Chapter 3

1. The presentation here is slightly anachronistic since *Aspects* predated the X-bar theory by a few years.

2. Earlier McCawley (1968) also proposed such a theory.

3. Starting in the late 1970s, Chomsky developed a theory of *principles and parameters*, where the principles are universal and the parameters are the few, simple ways that languages are assumed to be able to vary. Acquiring the syntax of a language then amounts to setting the parameters. The head parameter has two values: head before complements or head after complements. This parameter can be set on the basis of very simple data.

4. Though there were already suggestions that subcategorization is related to meaning.

5. See Grimshaw 1979, though, for a strong argument that both semantic selection and subcategorization are needed.

6. Embedded questions now become problematic, since they show *Wh*-Movement without Subject-Aux Inversion, as in (i).

(i) I wonder what John will buy

This problem still has not really been solved.

7. This is reminiscent of something in *Syntactic Structures*: adjoining *n't* to C (what we now call I) and then moving the whole complex to the front of the sentence by Subject-Aux Inversion. *n't* moves to the front because it is part of one big C (now I).

8. The other possibility is substitution for C. At the moment the distinction is irrelevant.

9. This was actually implicit in *LSLT* for certain movements, but it was now made explicit.

10. Reinhart introduced the notion *c-command* to characterize relative height: roughly, A c-commands B if and only if every X dominating A also dominates B.

11. In the appendix of Lasnik 1992 I discuss that incorrect prediction further. Pollock (1989) actually claims that the prediction is correct, but see Iatridou 1990 for an alternative treatment of the examples he gives.

12. Notice that by *re-raising* I simply mean raising of the verb after the affix has hopped onto it.

13. In "A Minimalist Program for Linguistic Theory" (1993), which we will eventually get to, Chomsky does introduce a notion that could provide an answer for this question. The notion is *Procrastinate:* Wait as long as possible to do a particular operation. In other words, Procrastinate says, "Don't do an operation overtly if you can possibly do it covertly."

14. An unchecked strong feature is thus something like a stranded affix.

15. In "Categories and Transformations" Chomsky proposes that one way to remedy the look-ahead property is to say this: it isn't that a strong feature that isn't checked is bad at PF; it's that a strong feature that isn't checked *immediately* is bad. See Lasnik 1999 for a survey of several approaches to feature strength.

16. Unlike Agr$_S$ versus Agr$_O$, or specifier, "auxiliary" isn't a relational notion. We don't tell whether something is an auxiliary verb by seeing if there are other verbs in a sentence; rather, we look at its lexical entry.

17. I have not talked much about how *Do*-Support fits into the latest versions of the theory. I think this also works much the way it does in *Syntactic Structures:* a stranded affixal I is spelled out as the relevant form of *do*. That seems the simplest theory now, just as it did 40 years ago.

18. The VP-ellipsis paradigm cannot be extended to the third class of auxiliary verbs, modals, because modals never occur bare, but only in finite form.

References

Berwick, Robert C. 1985. *The acquisition of syntactic knowledge*. Cambridge, Mass.: MIT Press.

Bošković, Željko. 1995. Principles of economy in nonfinite complementation. Doctoral dissertation, University of Connecticut, Storrs.

Bresnan, Joan. 1972. Theory of complementation in English syntax. Doctoral dissertation, MIT, Cambridge, Mass.

Chomsky, Noam. 1955. The logical structure of linguistic theory. Ms., Harvard University, Cambridge, Mass. [Revised 1956 version published in part by Plenum, New York, 1975; University of Chicago Press, 1985.]

Chomsky, Noam. 1957. *Syntactic structures*. The Hague: Mouton.

Chomsky, Noam. 1965. *Aspects of the theory of syntax*. Cambridge, Mass.: MIT Press.

Chomsky, Noam. 1970. Remarks on nominalization. In *Readings in English transformational grammar*, edited by Roderick A. Jacobs and Peter S. Rosenbaum, 184–221. Waltham, Mass.: Ginn. [Reprinted in *Studies on semantics in generative grammar*, 11–61. The Hague: Mouton, 1972.]

Chomsky, Noam. 1973. Conditions on transformations. In *A festschrift for Morris Halle*, edited by Stephen Anderson and Paul Kiparsky, 232–286. New York: Holt, Rinehart and Winston.

Chomsky, Noam. 1981. *Lectures on government and binding*. Dordrecht: Foris.

Chomsky, Noam. 1986. *Barriers*. Cambridge, Mass.: MIT Press.

Chomsky, Noam. 1991. Some notes on economy of derivation and representation. In *Principles and parameters in comparative grammar*, edited by Robert Freidin, 417–454. Cambridge, Mass.: MIT Press. [Reprinted in *The Minimalist Program*, 129–166. Cambridge, Mass.: MIT Press, 1995.]

Chomsky, Noam. 1993. A minimalist program for linguistic theory. In *The view from Building 20*, edited by Kenneth Hale and Samuel Jay Keyser, 1–52. Cambridge, Mass.: MIT Press. [Reprinted in *The Minimalist Program*, 167–217. Cambridge, Mass.: MIT Press, 1995.]

Chomsky, Noam. 1995. Categories and transformations. In *The Minimalist Program*, 219–394. Cambridge, Mass.: MIT Press.

Chomsky, Noam, and Morris Halle. 1968. *The sound pattern of English*. New York: Harper and Row.

Chomsky, Noam, and Howard Lasnik. 1977. Filters and control. *Linguistic Inquiry* 8, 425–504. [Reprinted in Howard Lasnik, *Essays on restrictiveness and learnability*, 42–124. Dordrecht: Kluwer, 1990.]

Chomsky, Noam, and Howard Lasnik. 1993. The theory of principles and parameters. In *Syntax: An international handbook of contemporary research*, vol. 1, edited by Joachim Jacobs, Arnim von Stechow, Wolfgang Sternefeld, and Theo Vennemann, 506–569. Berlin: Walter de Gruyter. [Reprinted in Noam Chomsky, *The Minimalist Program*, 13–127. Cambridge, Mass.: MIT Press, 1995.]

Crain, Stephen, and Mineharu Nakayama. 1987. Structure dependence in grammar formation. *Language* 63, 522–543.

Dell, François. 1981. On the learnability of optional phonological rules. *Linguistic Inquiry* 12, 31–37.

Emonds, Joseph. 1978. The verbal complex V′–V in French. *Linguistic Inquiry* 9, 151–175.

Fiengo, Robert. 1977. On trace theory. *Linguistic Inquiry* 8, 35–62.

Grimshaw, Jane. 1979. Complement selection and the lexicon. *Linguistic Inquiry* 10, 279–326.

Gruber, Jeffrey S. 1976. Studies in lexical relations. Amsterdam: North-Holland. [Doctoral dissertation, MIT, Cambridge, Mass., 1965.]

Harris, Zellig. 1952. Discourse analysis. *Language* 28, 18–23.

Harris, Zellig. 1957. Co-occurrence and transformation in linguistic analysis. *Language* 33, 283–340.

Huang, C.-T. James. 1982. Logical relations in Chinese and the theory of grammar. Doctoral dissertation, MIT, Cambridge, Mass.

Iatridou, Sabine. 1990. About Agr (P). *Linguistic Inquiry* 21, 551–577.

Klima, Edward S. 1964. Negation in English. In *The structure of language: Readings in the philosophy of language*, edited by Jerry A. Fodor and Jerrold J. Katz, 246–323. Englewood Cliffs, N.J.: Prentice-Hall.

Kuroda, S.-Y. 1988. Whether we agree or not: A comparative syntax of English and Japanese. In *Papers from the Second International Workshop on Japanese Syntax*, edited by William J. Poser, 103–143. Stanford, Calif.: CSLI Publications. [Distributed by Cambridge University Press.]

Lasnik, Howard. 1981. Restricting the theory of transformations: A case study. In *Explanation in linguistics*, edited by Norbert Hornstein and David Lightfoot,

152–173. London: Longmans. [Reprinted in *Essays on restrictiveness and learnability*, 125–145. Dordrecht: Kluwer, 1990.]

Lasnik, Howard. 1992. Case and expletives: Notes toward a parametric account. *Linguistic Inquiry* 23, 381–405.

Lasnik, Howard. 1995. Verbal morphology: *Syntactic Structures* meets the Minimalist Program. In *Evolution and revolution in linguistic theory: Essays in honor of Carlos Otero*, edited by Héctor Campos and Paula Kempchinsky, 251–275. Washington, D.C.: Georgetown University Press. [Reprinted in *Minimalist analysis*, 97–119. Oxford: Blackwell, 1999.]

Lasnik, Howard. 1999. On feature strength: Three minimalist approaches to overt movement. *Linguistic Inquiry* 30, 197–217.

Lasnik, Howard, and Joseph J. Kupin. 1977. A restrictive theory of transformational grammar. *Theoretical Linguistics* 4, 173–196. [Reprinted in Howard Lasnik, *Essays on restrictiveness and learnablity*, 17–41. Dordrecht: Kluwer, 1990.]

Lasnik, Howard, and Juan Uriagereka. 1988. *A course in GB syntax: Lectures on binding and empty categories*. Cambridge, Mass.: MIT Press.

May, Robert. 1977. The grammar of quantification. Doctoral dissertation, MIT, Cambridge, Mass.

McCawley, James D. 1968. Concerning the base component of a transformational grammar. *Foundations of Language* 4, 243–269.

McCawley, James D. 1992. A note on auxiliary verbs and language acquisition. *Journal of Linguistics* 28, 445–451.

Pesetsky, David. 1982. Paths and categories. Doctoral dissertation, MIT, Cambridge, Mass.

Pollock, Jean-Yves. 1989. Verb movement, Universal Grammar, and the structure of IP. *Linguistic Inquiry* 20, 365–424.

Reinhart, Tanya. 1976. The Syntactic domain of anaphora. Doctoral dissertation, MIT, Cambridge, Mass.

Rizzi, Luigi. 1990. *Relativized Minimality*. Cambridge, Mass.: MIT Press.

Roberts, Ian. 1991. Excorporation and minimality. *Linguistic Inquiry* 22, 209–218.

Rosenbaum, Peter S. 1967. *The grammar of English predicate complement constructions*. Cambridge, Mass.: MIT Press.

Ross, John Robert. 1967. Constraints on variables in syntax. Doctoral dissertation, MIT, Cambridge, Mass. [Published as *Infinite syntax!* Norwood, N.J.: Ablex (1986).]

Ross, John Robert. 1969a. Auxiliaries as main verbs. *Studies in Philosophical Linguistics* 1, 77–102.

Ross, John Robert. 1969b. Guess who? In *Papers from the Fifth Regional Meeting of the Chicago Linguistic Society*, edited by Robert I. Binnick et al., 252–286. Chicago Linguistic Society, University of Chicago, Chicago, Ill.

Stowell, Tim. 1981. Origins of phrase structure. Doctoral dissertation, MIT, Cambridge, Mass.

Travis, Lisa. 1984. Parameters and effects of word order variation. Doctoral dissertation, MIT, Cambridge, Mass.

Warner, Anthony. 1986. Ellipsis conditions and the status of the English copula. In *York papers in linguistics 3*, 87–107.

Watanabe, Akira. 1993. AGR-based Case theory and its interaction with the Ā-system. Doctoral dissertation, MIT, Cambridge, Mass.

Index

Adequacy, 20
  descriptive, 38, 39, 72
  explanatory, 39, 76, 115, 116, 119, 121, 123
Adjacency, 17, 80, 81, 86, 98, 103, 105, 113, 122–124, 187–188, 191–192, 194
  hierarchical, 187
  linear, 188, 192
Adjunction, 54, 62, 64, 66, 72, 75, 88–99, 93, 95, 96, 144, 147, 152, 156. *See also* Transformation, elementary
  left, 88, 62n8
  right, 62, 88, 93
Adverb (placement), 157, 165, 168
Affirmation Transformation (T17), 57, 75, 86, 98, 105, 109
Affixal. *See* Inflection, affixal
Affix Hopping (T20), 53–55, 59, 60–62, 72, 74n12, 78, 89, 90, 92, 93, 95, 96, 100, 101, 103, 104, 113, 122–124, 127, 140, 147, 153, 158, 163, 166–170, 172, 175, 179, 187, 194
  and adjacency, 80, 86
  as adjunction, 64, 66
  followed by raising, 168
  as head lowering, 153
  and main verbs, 155
  morphology of, 70
  and negation, 169–179
  obligatoriness of, 80, 115
  structural analysis of, 53, 57, 69
  structural change of, 53, 61
Agreement, 143, 144
  forced, 144
  in phi-features, 183
  Specifier-head, 143, 145
Anaphor, 158
A-over-A constraint, 90, 91, 93, 101, 147, 153, 155, 156

Autonomy of syntax, 186
Auxiliary, 7, 16, 35, 37, 38, 40, 41–49, 67, 79, 89, 134, 140, 141, 145, 146, 149, 150, 159, 161, 162, 165, 185, 187, 188, 191–193, 196, 199n22
Auxiliary Transformation (T20). *See* Affix Hopping

Bare verb, 47, 154, 192. *See also* Lexicalist vs. bare
Base component, 129, 130
Boolean combination, 57, 68, 106–107, 122, 149
Boolean condition on analyzability, 107–111, 124
  conjunction as, 110
  disjunction as, 109
  negation as, 108, 109, 110

C. *See* Symbol; Inflection
Category, 178
C-command, 158n10, 166, 200n10
Chain, 181
Checking, 183, 184, 185, 190, 191, 192, 193, 194, 200n14
Complement, 129, 130, 133. *See also* X-bar theory
Complementizer (CP), 142, 143, 144, 148
Compositionality, 197n8. *See also* Meaning
Conjunctive, 84
Constant term, 60, 116, 121
Constituency, 9, 10, 11, 28, 30, 33, 63, 76, 106, 107, 127. *See also* Structure dependence
  test, 9–11
Constituent structure. *See* Phrase marker
Coordination, 11. *See also* Constituency
Covert movement, 168, 172, 183, 184, 185, 187

Creative aspect of language, 3
Cyclicity, 130

Daughter, 197n5
D(eep)-Structure, 130, 160, 161, 164, 167, 178
Defective verb, 155. *See also* Modal
Deletion, 64, 157, 180, 181
  under identity, 108
  recoverability of, 108, 109, 173
  of VP (*see* VP ellipsis)
Dependency
  cross-serial, 48, 51, 65–66, 103–104
  global, 66
  nested, 48
  unbounded discontinuous, 16
Derivation, 13, 17, 19–21, 23, 25, 27–29, 48, 51, 55, 73, 132. *See also* Transformation
  equivalent, 19, 23, 24, 25, 29, 30, 32, 34, 49, 197n3
  more economical, 167
  nonequivalent, 24, 25, 26, 28
Derivational vs. inflectional morphology, 182, 190–191. *See also* Lexicalist Hypothesis
Derived constituent structure, 52. *See also* Constituency; Phrase marker, derived
Descriptive power, 19, 26, 107–108, 115
Dominate, 197n5
Do-Support (T21b), 81–85, 89, 91, 96–98, 102–105, 113, 120, 127, 141, 146, 153, 155, 163, 179, 180, 186, 193, 201n17
  as a last resort, 153, 155, 156
  structural analysis of, 81
  structural change of, 81
Driving force, 181

Economy, 167
Ellipsis, 157. *See also* VP ellipsis
Evaluation metric, 39, 40, 41, 68, 69, 70, 73, 109, 121, 122, 125, 128
Excorporation, 156
Extended Projection Principle (EPP), 134
Extraposition, 110, 186

Featural. *See* Inflection, featural
Finite state machine (Markov process), 12–18, 23
French, 150, 151, 157–159, 162, 165, 169–171, 173, 182, 183, 186, 188, 190, 191, 194

Graph theory, 22, 33, 58

Head, 129, 130, 136, 137, 145, 148. *See also* X-bar theory

Head movement, 143, 145, 147, 148, 150, 153, 158
  successive, 147
Head Movement Constraint (HMC), 146, 150–152, 154–156, 165, 169–171, 187, 188, 189, 193
Head parameter, 129, 132, 144, 200n3

Identity, 59, 108
I lowering to V, 153, 155, 157, 158. *See also* Affix Hopping
Imperative, 162, 194–195
Individual psychology, 2, 11
Infinity, 3, 4, 11–14, 19, 23, 39
Inflection (I, Infl), 137–139, 142, 143, 145–148, 151, 188
  affixal, 190–195
  in English, 159
  featural, 189, 190–195
  in French, 159
  split, 163, 170, 171, 173
Interrogative, 7, 8, 66, 99. *See also* Subject-Aux(iliary) Inversion
  yes/no question, 8, 16
Inversion, 6, 7, 66, 99, 148, 152
"Is a" relation, 25, 29, 30–33, 69
Island, 157, 167, 168
  Wh-island constraint, 167
I-to-C movement, 144, 145, 147, 155

Knowledge of language, 1–3, 11, 12, 38, 39, 40

Labeled bracketing, 8, 9
Language acquisition (learnability), 6, 8, 39, 40, 107, 111, 114, 115, 120, 136, 155, 200n3
Last resort, 153, 155, 156, 157. *See also* Minimalism
Lexicalist Hypothesis, 182
Lexicalist vs. bare, 182, 187, 188, 191, 194
Lexicon, 130, 131, 132, 136, 155, 190
Logical Form (LF), 186–187. *See also* Covert movement
Lowering, 76, 153, 155, 157–159, 172, 173, 178, 182, 183, 188, 192

Main verb, 36, 37, 38, 44, 49, 159, 188, 191, 192
Meaning (interpretation), 5, 6, 28, 43, 94, 101, 134, 160, 161, 167, 171, 186, 197n8. *See also* LF; Scope
Minimalism, 153, 181–182
Mirror image language, 14, 16. *See also* Finite state machine

Modal, 36, 37, 43, 45, 48, 49, 91, 102, 138, 154, 155, 161, 162
Monostring, 31, 33, 34
Morphophonemics (morphology), 69, 70, 74, 81, 91, 94, 100, 101, 153, 155, 159, 163, 182, 183, 192, 198n7

N't/not, 126–127
Natural class, 111, 125, 138
Negation Transformation (T16), 56, 75, 86–88, 91–93, 95, 96, 98–100, 102, 105, 109, 149, 150, 169, 172, 190, 191, 193, 195
  as adjunction to a term, 64
  structural analysis of, 56, 86
Negative data. *See* Negative evidence
Negative evidence, 115, 118, 119, 121. *See also* Language acquisition
Number Transformation (T15), 53–55, 57, 59–61, 62, 64, 72, 73, 77, 79, 92, 94, 102, 104, 130
  structural analysis of, 53, 59
  structural change of, 53, 60

Overgeneration, 14, 80, 85, 86, 113, 114, 116, 119, 120, 121, 126

Passive Transformation (T12), 57, 59, 64, 65, 100n19, 115, 145, 199n19
Permutation, 64, 66, 75, 99, 142, 143. *See also* Transformation, Elementary
  cyclic, 42
Phonology
  explanation in, 17, 11, 118, 122, 178, 198n12
Phrase marker (PM), 30, 31, 33, 34, 48, 52, 58, 65
  derived, 51, 52, 59, 61
  initial, 51, 65, 132
  reduced (RPM), 33
Phrase structure grammar, 16–20, 24, 28–30, 48, 129
  context-free, 16, 29, 34, 129
  context-sensitive, 17
Phrase Structure rule, 17, 19, 21, 26–28, 32, 34, 48, 51, 54, 61, 70, 104, 128, 132
  context-free, 54, 104, 129
  context-sensitive, 54, 104
Phrase Structure tree, collapsed, 21–26, 32, 33, 48
Positive data. *See* Positive evidence
Positive evidence, 115, 118, 119. *See also* Language acquisition
Primary linguistic data (PLD), 39–40. *See also* Language acquisition
Principles-and-Parameters, 200n3

Procrastinate, 169n13, 183–186, 200n13
Projection, 178
Projection Principle, 134–135
Pronominalization, 9–11. *See also* Constituency
Proper Binding Condition, 158, 165, 167

Quantificational statement, 107, 108–110, 124
Question forming, 8

Readjustment rule, 101
Recursion, 17, 19
  in the base, 23, 24, 130
Relativized Minimality, 148, 191
Rewrite rule, 16–19, 21, 26, 32, 48, 72, 87
Ross's problem, 69, 70, 109, 112, 114, 125, 126, 135, 138, 161. *See also* Natural class
Rule. *See* Transformation

Scope, 101–102, 160. *See also* Meaning
Selection, 112n22, 126, 129, 130, 132–134, 134n5, 136, 145
  c(ategorial)-, 133
  s(emantic)-, 133
Selectional restriction, 70, 132, 133. *See also* Selection
Semantic bootstrapping, 134. *See also* Language Acquisition
Sequence of tense, 43, 138
Set theory, 29, 31, 33, 34, 58, 63, 64, 75
[Σ, F] grammar. *See* Phrase structure grammar, context-free
Sister, 197n5
Sloppy identity, 196. *See also* VP ellipsis
Specifier, 144, 145, 148. *See also* X-bar theory
Split Infl, 163. *See also* Inflection
  AgrO as part of, 170–171
  AgrS as part of, 173
Stranded affix, 83, 89, 123, 124, 153, 157, 169, 181, 182, 191, 194, 200n14
  Filter, 123, 169
Strength, 166, 200n15
Structural ambiguity, 22, 25–29, 43, 114
Structural analysis, 56, 68–70, 107, 108, 119, 142
  formalization of, 57–59
  satisfaction of, 59
Structural change, 56, 59, 61, 119, 142
  formalization of, 64
Structure dependence, 5, 8, 51, 76, 124, 127, 128, 149. *See also* Constituency
  non-structure-dependent error, 8
Subcategorization, 112n22, 126, 130, 133, 134n5, 136

Subject, 8, 9, 16, 37, 38, 65, 134, 143
Subject-Aux(iliary) Inversion (T18), 56, 57, 66, 73–75, 78–80, 86, 98–101, 105, 107, 112, 127, 141–145, 150. *See also* I-to-C movement
  as permutation, 64, 89, 99
  structural analysis of, 56
  structural change of, 75
Subset principle, 117, 118, 121
S(urface)-structure, 130, 167
Swedish, 186, 187
Symbol
  C, 41, 48, 60, 62, 69, 87, 89, 96, 137, 146
  initial, 16, 17, 48
  nonterminal, 17–20, 23, 24, 26, 30–32, 57, 79, 106, 124
  terminal, 17, 23, 24, 29, 30, 31, 33, 48, 57, 63, 79, 81, 106, 124

T19, 66, 144
Term, 56–58, 64, 68, 106, 107, 124, 125
Thematic role. *See* Theta-role
Theta-Criterion, 135, 160, 163, 164, 178, 179
Theta-grid, 135
Theta-role, 134, 160–162, 165
  agent, 135
  assigned to main verb, 159
  patient, 135, 137
  theme, 135
Topicalization, 10, 11, 91. *See also* Constituency
Trace (theory), 157, 158, 161, 165, 166, 169, 171, 173, 179
Transformation, 3, 8, 24, 51–56, 58, 63, 66, 67, 69, 72, 73, 76, 78, 84, 87
  elementary, 64
  generalized (GT), 23, 24, 130
  lexical insertion, 26, 130
  obligatory, 59, 65, 77, 80, 105, 114, 115, 119–124, 127
  optional, 41, 59, 65, 75, 77, 114–116, 119, 120, 123, 124
  ordering of, 64, 65, 115, 116, 119, 120, 121, 123, 127
  singulary, 130
  structure-preserving, 62, 63
Transitive verb, 125, 126, 135
Tree pruning, 76

Undergeneration, 85, 113, 114, 119, 120

Variable, 57, 59, 106, 116, 117, 121, 128
  placement, 116, 121

Verb movement. *See* Head movement, V-to-I raising
VP-ellipsis, 108, 195–196
V-to-I raising, 147, 151, 155, 157, 163, 167

Wh-movement, 144, 145, 167
Word boundary, 53, 62, 67, 81–85, 96–98, 107
Word Boundary Transformation (T21a), 81, 83, 120
  involving negative statements, 107
  obligatoriness of, 84
  structural analysis of, 81
  structural change of, 81

X-bar schema, 128
X-bar theory, 128, 130, 136, 139, 142, 145, 149–151, 178
  complement in, 129, 138, 144
  extended, 137
  head in, 129
  head-complement relations in, 131
  specifier in, 138, 144

Zero morpheme, 44, 72, 192

Current Studies in Linguistics
Samuel Jay Keyser, general editor

1. *A Reader on the Sanskrit Grammarians*, J. F. Staal, editor
2. *Semantic Interpretation in Generative Grammar*, Ray Jackendoff
3. *The Structure of the Japanese Language*, Susumu Kuno
4. *Speech Sounds and Features*, Gunnar Fant
5. *On Raising: One Rule of English Grammar and Its Theoretical Implications*, Paul M. Postal
6. *French Syntax: The Transformational Cycle*, Richard S. Kayne
7. *Pāṇini as a Variationist*, Paul Kiparsky, S. D. Joshi, editor
8. *Semantics and Cognition*, Ray Jackendoff
9. *Modularity in Syntax: A Study of Japanese and English*, Ann Kathleen Farmer
10. *Phonology and Syntax: The Relation between Sound and Structure*, Elisabeth O. Selkirk
11. *The Grammatical Basis of Linguistic Performance: Language Use and Acquisition*, Robert C. Berwick and Amy S. Weinberg
12. *Introduction to the Theory of Grammar*, Henk van Riemsdijk and Edwin Williams
13. *Word and Sentence Prosody in Serbocroatian*, Ilse Lehiste and Pavle Ivić
14. *The Representation of (In)definiteness*, Eric J. Reuland and Alice G. B. ter Meulen, editors
15. *An Essay on Stress*, Morris Halle and Jean-Roger Vergnaud
16. *Language and Problems of Knowledge: The Managua Lectures*, Noam Chomsky
17. *A Course in GB Syntax: Lectures on Binding and Empty Categories*, Howard Lasnik and Juan Uriagereka
18. *Semantic Structures*, Ray Jackendoff
19. *Events in the Semantics of English: A Study in Subatomic Semantics*, Terence Parsons
20. *Principles and Parameters in Comparative Grammar*, Robert Freidin, editor
21. *Foundations of Generative Syntax*, Robert Freidin
22. *Move α: Conditions on Its Application and Output*, Howard Lasnik and Mamoru Saito

23. *Plurals and Events*, Barry Schein
24. *The View from Building 20: Essays in Linguistics in Honor of Sylvain Bromberger*, Kenneth Hale and Samuel Jay Keyser, editors
25. *Grounded Phonology*, Diana Archangeli and Douglas Pulleyblank
26. *The Magic of a Common Language: Jakobson, Mathesius, Trubetzkoy, and the Prague Linguistic Circle*, Jindřich Toman
27. *Zero Syntax: Experiencers and Cascades*, David Pesetsky
28. *The Minimalist Program*, Noam Chomsky
29. *Three Investigations of Extraction*, Paul M. Postal
30. *Acoustic Phonetics*, Kenneth N. Stevens
31. *Principle B, VP Ellipsis, and Interpretation in Child Grammar*, Rosalind Thornton and Kenneth Wexler
32. *Working Minimalism*, Samuel Epstein and Norbert Hornstein, editors
33. Syntactic Structures *Revisited: Contemporary Lectures on Classic Transformational Theory*, Howard Lasnik, with Marcela Depiante and Arthur Stepanov

Examples of English Phrase Structure and Transformational Rules from *Syntactic Structures*

The following phrase structure rules appear on page 111 of *Syntactic Structures*.

Σ: # Sentence #[1]

F: 1. Sentence $\rightarrow$ NP + VP
   2. VP $\quad\rightarrow$ Verb + NP
   3. NP $\quad\rightarrow$ NP$_{\text{sing}}$
   $\qquad\qquad\quad$ NP$_{\text{pl}}$
   4. NP$_{\text{sing}} \rightarrow$ T + N + $\varnothing$
   5. NP$_{\text{pl}} \quad\rightarrow$ T + N + S[2]
   6. T $\quad\rightarrow$ *the*
   7. N $\quad\rightarrow$ *man, ball*, etc.
   8. Verb $\rightarrow$ Aux + V
   9. V $\quad\rightarrow$ *hit, take, walk, read*, etc.
   10. Aux $\rightarrow$ C(M) (*have* + *en*) (*be* + *ing*)
   11. M $\quad\rightarrow$ *will, can, may, shall, must*

The following transformational rules, which appear on pages 112–113 of *Syntactic Structures*, are discussed in this book. Each is given with its *Syntactic Structures* name and, where applicable, the nickname by which it is generally known and under which it is discussed here. (SA = structural analysis; SC = structural change)

12. *Passive* (optional)
    SA: NP – Aux – V – NP
    SC: $X_1 - X_2 - X_3 - X_4 \rightarrow X_4 - X_2 + be + en - X_3 - by + X$

15. *Number Transformation* (obligatory)
    SA: X – C – Y
    SC: C $\rightarrow$ $\begin{cases} \text{S in the context NP}_{\text{sing}} \underline{\quad} \\ \varnothing \text{ in other contexts} \\ past \text{ in any context} \end{cases}$

16. T_{not} *"Negation Transformation"* (optional)
    SA: $\begin{cases} \text{NP} - \text{C} - \text{V} \ldots \\ \text{NP} - \text{C} + \text{M} - \ldots \\ \text{NP} - \text{C} + have - \ldots \\ \text{NP} - \text{C} + be - \ldots \end{cases}$ [3]
    SC: $X_1 - X_2 - X_3 \rightarrow X_1 - X_2 + n't - X_3$

17. T_A *"Affirmation"* (optional)
    SA: same as 16
    SC: $X_1 - X_2 - X_3 \rightarrow X_1 - X_2 + A - X_3$

18. T_q *"Subject-Aux Inversion"* (optional)
    SA: same as 16
    SC: $X_1 - X_2 - X_3 \rightarrow X_2 - X_1 - X_3$

19. T_{w1} *"Wh-Movement"* (optional and conditional on T_q)
    SA: X – NP – Y (X or Y may be null)
    SC: same as 18

20. *Auxiliary Transformation "Affix Hopping"* (obligatory)
    SA: X – "Af" – "v" – Y (where "Af" is any C or is *en* or *ing*; "v" is any M or V, or *have* or *be*)
    SC: $X_1 - X_2 - X_3 - X_4 \rightarrow X_1 - X_3 - X_2 \ \# - X_4$

21a. *Word Boundary Transformation* (obligatory)[4]
    SA: X – Y (where X ≠ "v" or Y ≠ "Af")
    SC: $X_1 - X_2 \rightarrow X_1 - \# \ X_2$

21b. *Do-Transformation "Do-Support"* (obligatory)
    SA: # – "Af"
    SC: $X_1 - X_2 \rightarrow X_1 - do + X_2$

[1] For brevity, S is used in this book rather than *Sentence*.
[2] *s* is used in this book rather than *S* to avoid confusion with the abbreviation S for *Sentence*.
[3] "V..." (for example) means 'V followed by anything at all'; it is equivalent to $V + X$ or $V \ X$. The notation in *Syntactic Structures* is somewhat inconsistent on this point.
[4] Transformations 21a and 21b are both numbered 21 in *Syntactic Structures*.